"People are just as wonderful as sun
When I look at a sunset, I don't fin
the orange a little on the right-hand
purple along the base, and use a litt
colour." I don't do that. I don't try to
it with awe as it unfolds. **-Carl Rogers**

Copyright © 2024 Claire Banks All rights reserved

No part of this book may be reproduced, or stored in a retrieval system, or transmitted in any form or by any means, electronic, mechanical, photocopying, recording, or otherwise, without express written permission of the author Claire Banks.

Cover photo by: Miguel Bruna on Unsplash

ISBN- 9798340343840

www.centredmindscounselling.co.uk

This book details my experience on the subject matter. The author does not guarantee the same outcomes they have experienced for the purchaser or reader of this book.

All attempts have been made to verify the information at the time of publication and the correct links, and the author does not assume any responsibility for errors, omissions, or other interpretations of the subject matter. The purchaser or reader of this book assumes responsibility for the use of this material and information. The author assumes no responsibility or liability on behalf of any purchaser or reader of this book.

NAILING COUNSELLING TRAINING

A NEWBIE'S EXPERIENCE OF BECOMING A QUALIFIED INTEGRATIVE COUNSELLOR

CLAIRE BANKS

Acknowledgements

I would like to express my deep gratitude to James, who became my unofficial book editor. When I recall the first draft I sent him—years of planning and visualising condensed into a manuscript that was, admittedly, utterly chaotic - it's clear how much this book has been transformed. Thanks to James's input, clarity emerged and this final version far exceeds my early expectations.

To Sarah, when I confided in you about my thoughts of writing a book based on my counselling training experience, your encouragement was exactly what I needed to believe this book idea was worthwhile.

To my family, who have been encouraging and supportive. I cannot thank you enough.

These past few years of undergoing counselling training and establishing my own business have been both challenging and daunting. The constant changes have pushed me to learn more about myself, my resilience, and the new meaning I am discovering in life. I was overlooked in school, dismissed, and left without any qualifications. Yet, I have turned my circumstances around, and you can too. Do not allow others to define your worth. I stand as living proof that you can achieve your goals and create the life you desire.

Aim high! Claire XX

Author Biography

After spending over 25 years working with software and hardware in various industries, where I honed my people management, listening, problem-solving, and communication skills, I realised that my true calling was to work more directly with individuals on a personal level. This led me to undertake counselling training - which I nailed - resulting in obtaining a Diploma in Integrative Counselling.

I am now working successfully in private practice in the UK, specialising in short and long-term counselling for adults aged 18+ at www.centredmindscounselling.co.uk

Contents

~ INTRODUCTION ~ 1
- How To Use This Book — 2
- Notes To Bear In Mind — 3
- Personal Experience With Mental Health — 3
- What I Wished I Knew Before Counselling Training — 4

~ CHAPTER 1 ~ FINDING A COURSE 7
- Ofqual Recognised Courses — 8
- Professional Standards Authority (PSA) — 8
- Membership Organisations — 9
- Accredited vs Non-Accredited Courses — 9
- Mandatory Personal Counselling — 11
- Which Route To Take? — 12
- Top Tips — 13

~ CHAPTER 2 ~ COUNSELLING BASICS - LEVEL 1 17
- Introduction To Counselling — 18
- Humanistic Approach — 18
- Check-in / Check-out — 18
- Group Contract — 18
- Client Counselling Contract — 19
- Intake — 19
- Carl Rogers 3 Core Counselling Skills — 20
  - Empathy — 20
  - Congruence — 20
  - Unconditional Positive Regard (UPR) — 20
- Triads — 21
- Non-Verbal Communication (NVC) — 22

- Active Listening — 22
- Reflections — 23
- Paraphrasing — 23
- Clarifying — 24
- Silences — 25
- Immediacy — 25
- Summarising — 26
- Top Tips — 26

~ CHAPTER 3 ~ PERSONAL AWARENESS-LEVEL 2 ... 30

- Counselling Session Structure — 31
  - Beginnings — 31
  - Middle — 32
  - Endings — 33
- Ethical Framework — 35
- Self-disclosure — 36
- Self-awareness — 38
- Self-care — 39
- The Johari Window — 39
- *Maslow's Hierarchy Of Needs* — 41
- Research Project — 43
- Assessments — 43
- Top Tips — 44

~ CHAPTER 4 ~ THEORY OVERLOAD – LEVEL 3 48

- Process Group — 49
- Humanistic Models — 50
  - Carl Rogers - Person-Centred Approach (PCA) — 50
  - Irvin Yalom - Existentialism — 51

- o   Roberto Assagioli - Psychosynthesis   51
- o   Laura and Fritz Perls - Gestalt   52
- Non-Humanistic Models   53
  - o   Aaron Beck - Cognitive Behavioural Therapy (CBT)   53
  - o   Albert Ellis - Rational Emotive Behavioural Therapy (REBT)   54
  - o   Sigmund Freud – Psychodynamic   55
  - o   Carl Jung- Analytical Psychology   57
  - o   Donald Winnicott   58
  - o   John Bowlby   59
  - o   Schema Therapy   60
- Theory Round-up   61
- Assessments   62
- Top Tips   63

~ CHAPTER 5 ~ THE FINAL YEAR – LEVEL 4.............. 67
- Children & Young People (CYP)   68
- Differences And Diversity   69
- Ethics And Morals Revisited   71
- Class Placement Supervision   72
- Assessments   74
- Top Tips   75

~ CHAPTER 6 ~ PERSONAL COUNSELLING 78

~ CHAPTER 7 ~ 100 HOUR PLACEMENT – LEVEL 4 ... 85
- Preparing For Placement   86
- Find Out About Your Placement   87

- Social Media Presence — 89
- My Placement — 89
- Counselling Intake — 90
- Contracting — 91
- Safeguarding — 92
  - Breaking Confidentiality — 93
  - Safety Plan/Box — 93
  - Attempted Suicide — 94
  - Self-Harming — 94
  - Safeguarding Others — 95
- Awareness Of Time — 95
- First Client, First Hour — 96
  - Invite The Client To Start — 97
  - Being Door Knobbed — 97
  - One Hour Down! — 98
- That 10 Minute Warning — 98
- Are you sitting comfortably? — 99
- Communication Mediums — 100
- What Is The Client's Idea Of Counselling? — 100
- Client Notes — 101
- Working With Multiple Clients — 101
- That's Rude! — 102
- Being Late For Your Client — 103
- The Client Needs To Engage In Counselling — 103
- When Clients Have Nothing To Say — 105
- Planning Goes Out The Window — 105
- Creativity — 106

- Stones … 106
- Picture Cards … 107
- Fidget Toys … 107
- Drawing … 108
- Masks … 109
- Nesting Dolls … 109
- Conversation starter cubes … 109
- Emotion wheels … 110
- Distractions … 111
- My Tinder Alert System … 111
- Swearing Clients … 112
- Did Not Attend (DNA) … 112
- Where Are Your Clients? … 113
- Supervision … 113
  - Supervision/Client Ratio … 113
  - Get A Great Supervisor … 114
  - Peer Supervision … 115
- My Issues Coming Up…. Again! … 116
- Being Used By A Client … 117
- Asking For Advice … 118
- Bring It Into The Room … 118
- Recognising A Client's Parent … 119
- Dealing With Parents/Primary Caregivers … 120
- Dealing With Other Agencies … 121
- Client Gifts … 122
- Theory Coming Into Play … 123

- Anger Issues … 124
- Counting Down The One Hundred Placement Hours … 125
- Endings … 126
- Client Issues I Worked With … 127
- Placement Admin … 129
- My Self-Care … 129

~ CHAPTER 8 ~ POST-QUALIFYING CHANGES … 133

- Where Am I Now? … 134
- Looking Back … 135
- How Have I Changed? … 135
- Relationships … 137
  - Myself … 137
  - Family … 138
  - Existing Friendships … 138
  - New Friends … 139
  - Significant Other … 139
- Sitting With A Client … 140

~ CHAPTER 9 ~ USEFUL TRAINING RESOURCES … 142

- Digital … 143
- Books … 143
- My Favourite Books … 144
- Author's Note … 147

~ REFERENCES ~ … 148

~ Introduction ~

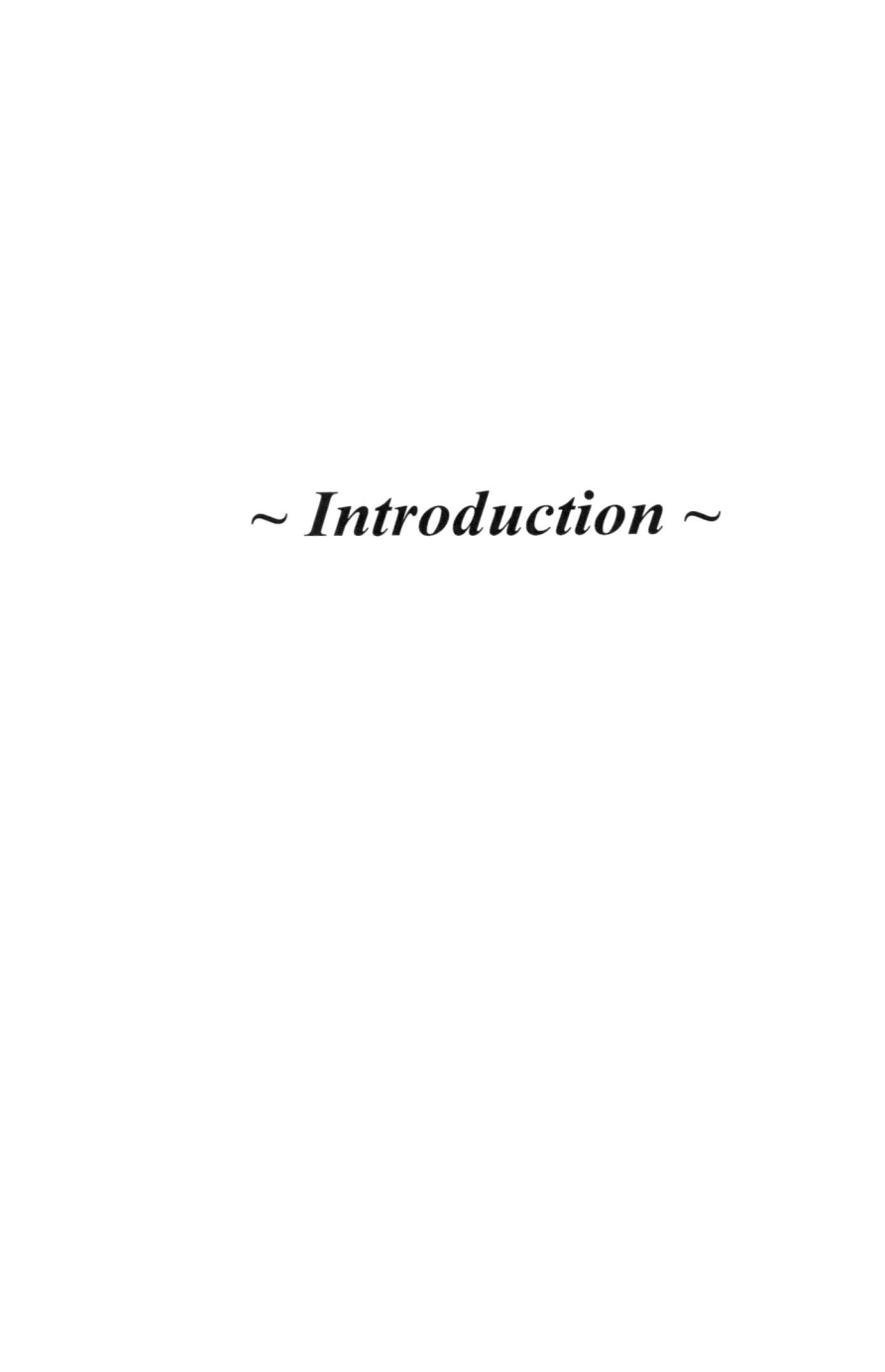

NAILING COUNSELLING TRAINING

A warm welcome and hello to you.

If you are reading this book then it is likely that you are thinking about undertaking counselling training to perhaps improve communication skills or become a qualified counsellor.

I was inspired to write this book as I embarked on my journey into counselling training and writing reflective notes to see how I might change during the training process. I could not find other books that captured this experience, so thought I would write about my own experiences that other people may find useful.

So, who is this book for? Well, it is for anyone who is thinking about taking that first step into studying an *Integrative* counselling course, or who is already on their own counselling journey. I would like to share my experience so you gain an understanding of what might be coming, what knowledge you might need, and how this newbie dealt with it all.

Integrative - *Combining different counselling approaches and techniques to create a flexible, personal counselling approach for a client.*

This book offers tips on choosing a counselling course provider and explores learning at various levels, including basic skills, counselling models, theories, ethics, the 100-hour placement undertaken during Level 4, and more. It concludes with a section on what has changed for me, and a list of helpful resources to support you on your counselling training journey.

I have included some reflective prompts throughout that might be useful to pause and reflect on the content. Personal reflection is likely to be interwoven throughout different counselling courses, so it is good to become familiar with this. I have added a Notes section to the end of the chapters to record any reflections or other notes that spring to mind as you read this book. However, this is only available in the paperback version, so apologies to any ebook readers.

At times, I found the counselling training to be an extremely bumpy ride, full of difficulties and challenges, but also positive experiences which have led to me changing my life for the better. I was ready to throw the towel in at one desperate point, but I persisted and powered through.

That's why I am writing this book.

REFLECTION POINT

What has led you to undertake a counselling course?

How To Use This Book

I have structured this book to make it simple to skip to sections that might be of interest at any given time. For example, if you are a newbie to the counselling world you might want to get a head-start on the core counselling skills or become familiar with the different counselling theories that might come up.

Alternatively, if you are further into your counselling training you may want to go straight to the placement section. At my Level 4 Diploma presentation evening, a group of students at

Level 3 and first-year Level 4 asked lots of questions about my experience of the 100-hour placement and no questions about the coursework they had coming up.

Notes To Bear In Mind

This book is written from my frame of reference as I experienced counselling training. Your training course and experiences are unlikely to match mine.

Not all courses will cover the same material or to the same depth. With that in mind, I have briefly documented my key learning across the counselling training levels, including the Placement section. Consider these areas a jumping-off point you might want to do a deep dive into if they have piqued your interest.

I have refrained from describing client conversations in detail to retain confidentiality and anonymity. Where I felt there was a point to make, I have been general.

This book is not intended as a tutorial in counselling and it will not tell you how to pass any counselling coursework or exams.

Personal Experience With Mental Health

My drive to enter the counselling profession is fuelled by my own experience of being badly let down by mental health professionals when I was younger. Although I cannot make it so, I do not want anyone else to experience such unprofessional and uncaring interactions at the point when care is needed the most. If I can help just one person when they need it, then I will be privileged and humble to have been there for them.

I had taken an overdose of pills in my late teens. This was a serious intention to end my life. After being treated in A&E I spent the night being monitored on a ward. In the morning, a nurse informed me that I needed to go into a nearby office, but did not inform me as to why.

I cannot recall if the person in the office was a psychiatrist or other mental health specialist. What I do recall is that they made me stand and wait until they had finished their phone call regarding when they would next play golf. This person then referred to me by the wrong name. Then they said the following:

"I know you know what you did was stupid, and that you won't do it again. Isn't that right?"

So of course, I agreed. I wanted to get out of that office and away from that person. I felt bewildered. My attempt to take my own life was buried deep down, never to be spoken about. I did not get the help I so clearly needed. I am glad I am alive today and am grateful to those who saved my life that night.

What I Wished I Knew Before Counselling Training

I went into counselling training having no real understanding of how my life might change, or about job prospects at the end of counselling training. Here are some things I wished I had known before starting.

1. I didn't realise quite how expensive counselling training would be, especially when you factor in supervision and placement costs.

NAILING COUNSELLING TRAINING

2. No two counselling sessions will be the same, do not compare yourself to your peers.

3. I didn't realise how lonely counselling would be.

4. You are likely to change as a person and lose people from your life.

5. I am now in a much better place in myself as a result of counselling training.

6. Finding a job that pays the bills will be tough. It seems everyone wants volunteer counsellors.

7. Not all tutors, supervisors or counsellors are nice! I assumed by the very nature of the job they would be.

8. A counselling training organisation can be harmful.

9. You cannot "fix" clients.

10. Expect to confront your own issues.

11. Not everyone will understand your path.

12. There is lots of admin involved.

13. Buckle up for a ride on the emotional rollercoaster.

NOTES

~ *Chapter 1* ~
Finding A Course

I wanted to find a counselling training organisation that offered at a minimum, the Level 4 Diploma in Counselling. The Level 4 Diploma is recognised as someone having completed training to certain standards and is deemed competent to work as a counsellor in the UK. Currently, counselling is not a government-regulated profession and the titles 'counsellor,' 'therapist,' and 'psychotherapist' are not protected titles. This effectively means that there is no law against anyone calling themselves by these titles.

I found searching for a course quite confusing. Search results would return with words such as 'accredited,' 'regulated,' and 'endorsed' and I did not understand what these meant.

Ofqual Recognised Courses

The Office of Qualifications and Examinations Regulation (Ofqual) reports to Parliament. Information about Ofqual can be found on the UK Government website.

The Ofqual recognition provides confidence that the training organisation is competent to offer the qualification.

Check if your course is regulated by Ofqual. Your course provider should be able to tell you or check directly with Ofqual.

Professional Standards Authority (PSA)

The PSA is an accredited register for certain services not regulated by law. Counselling in the UK is regulated by the PSA for Health and Social Care.

Information about the PSA can be found on the UK Government website.

"The Professional Standards Authority for Health and Social Care (the PSA) promotes the health, safety and wellbeing of patients, service users and the public. It does this by improving the regulation of people who work in health and social care and running the Accredited Registers programme for roles not regulated by law. The PSA is an independent body, accountable to the UK Parliament." - **Gov.uk.**

Membership Organisations

Counselling membership organisations can apply to be on the PSA register. A reason to join a membership organisation on the PSA register upon qualifying as a counsellor is that it shows potential clients or employers you have undertaken a certain standard of counselling training, more likely to be competent, trustworthy, and take action to protect the public when necessary, and meet the PSA standard overall.

Membership may also offer access to free or discounted Continuous Professional Development, counselling webinars, magazines, networking events, etc.

These membership organisations are voluntary, you do not have to join one.

Accredited vs Non-Accredited Courses

Some counselling courses are accredited, and some are not. Accredited means that the course has been approved by a membership organisation as meeting certain standards.

Accredited courses might be more expensive, so compare costs and shop around.

The main couple of membership organisations that accredit courses in the UK are:

- British Association for Counselling and Psychotherapy (BACP).

- National Counselling & Psychotherapy Society (NCPS).

Undertaking an accredited course usually means that upon successful completion, a qualified practitioner can join the associated membership organisation at a certain level. For instance, if your course were BACP accredited, you would automatically join the BACP as a registered member. This means potential clients would be able to search for you on BACP's publicly searchable database of counsellors who meet the BACP quality standards.

It is not the end of the world if the counselling course is not accredited. You can still apply to join whichever membership organisation you want if you meet their joining criteria (usually a minimum number of face-to-face tutor hours, 100-hour supervised placement, and evidence of a Diploma certificate). There may also be an exam or similar to complete as further evidence you qualify for their membership standard. For instance, if your counselling course was not accredited by the BACP, you can join as an individual member, and then sit an exam within 2 years of joining to become a registered member. This is what I did.

NAILING COUNSELLING TRAINING

Taking an accredited course does not mean you will become an accredited counsellor upon qualification, these are two different things. Check with your preferred membership organisation what the different counsellor levels are and what you need to achieve to reach them, if this is what you want. For instance, an accredited counsellor will need evidence they have performed a certain number of supervised client hours, a certain number of years' experience in counselling, and possibly complete a case study or similar to evidence their work meets higher standards.

Mandatory Personal Counselling

There is likely to be a mandatory element to your course of having personal counselling. The number of required hours can vary, my course required 10 hours. I started mine in the break between Level 3 and Level 4.

Here are a few reasons why this is important to undertake during counselling training:

- **Self-Awareness and Personal Growth:** Personal counselling helps trainee counsellors gain deep insight into their emotions, triggers, and unresolved issues. Self-awareness is essential in counselling because it allows counsellors to separate their personal experiences and biases from their clients' experiences, leading to more objective and effective support.

- **Dealing with Emotional Impact:** Counsellors often deal with heavy emotional content from clients, which can lead to emotional strain or burnout. Personal counselling helps trainees learn how to manage their mental and emotional health, ensuring they are resilient and can provide sustainable care to others. Continuing to have counselling at times may be beneficial for these reasons once qualified, ensuring that you are mentally and emotionally healthy.

- **Understanding the Client Perspective:** Trainees gain insight into the client's experience of vulnerability, trust-building, and emotional disclosure, which informs their approach to creating a safe and supportive space for clients.

- **Fostering Ethical Practice:** Counselling involves handling sensitive, confidential information and requires strong ethical principles. Personal counselling encourages trainees to reflect on and uphold these ethical standards in their professional work.

Which Route To Take?

I chose to study for a Level 4 Integrative Diploma in Counselling, completing Level 2 to Level 4 with the same training provider. This course was initially accredited by the NCPS, but before commencing Level 3 the training organisation and the NCPS parted ways. A new awarding body for the course was partnered with who was endorsed by Ofqual, so I decided to stick with the training provider. Therefore, I effectively ended up studying a non-accredited counselling course.

My training consisted of the following levels:

Level 1 Introduction to Counselling.

Level 2 Certificate in Counselling Skills (Beginner).

NAILING COUNSELLING TRAINING

Level 3 (fast track) Certificate in Counselling Skills (Intermediate Level).

Level 4 (fast track) Diploma in Counselling. This level is equivalent to a first-year bachelor's degree.

Fast track means lessons are completed at a minimum, one day per week over one year as opposed to a few hours per week. There will likely be some set weekends that you will need to attend also.

Check that your counselling course provides the required number of face-to-face tutoring hours. There are a lot of counselling courses advertised to the higher Certificate or Diploma Levels that are online and claim you would be qualified. It is unlikely that you would be professionally trained and would not meet the criteria to join a membership organisation if the course were online.

Other routes to becoming a qualified counsellor are conversion courses for existing applicable degrees, which have equivalence to the higher Counselling Levels:

Level 5 = Equivalent to a Foundation degree.

Level 6 = Equivalent to an Honours degree.

Level 7 = Equivalent to a Master's degree.

Ensure that the 100-hour placement part is included in your course if you choose this route.

Top Tips

1. Check out the training provider for any online reviews.

2. Have a chat with the training provider before signing up to answer questions you may have.

3. Ask about the complaints process.

4. Check if the tutors are qualified counsellors.

5. If in-house supervision as part of the placement experience is included, check the supervisors are qualified.

6. Check there are frequent tutor observations of skills practice.

7. Check if the training provider conducts interviews before accepting students onto the counselling course.

8. Make sure you can commit to the course, as there is usually a minimum attendance level. Drop below this and you might fail.

9. Check if your assessments require video or audio recording when you start working with clients. Your placement and clients will need to agree to this.

10. Consider all costs. Things like personal counselling, books, laptops, supervision etc.

11. Check that your training provider offers what is needed to join membership organisations, e.g., the required number of face-to-face teaching hours and 100-hour placement.

12. Some course providers may accept advanced learner loans, check the UK Government website for information.

NAILING COUNSELLING TRAINING

13. If doing a fast-track course be mindful about completing the 100-hour placement over one year. Check how long your course provider gives you to complete this.

14. Consider everything you have going on. I balanced part-time work, two Diploma courses, my volunteer bereavement support role, major house renovations, and life's challenges—without realising the emotional toll of counselling training. It was tough, and I would not do it this way again.

NOTES

~ *Chapter 2* ~
Counselling Basics - Level 1

Introduction To Counselling

Level 1 may also be known as an Introduction to Counselling course and is shorter than the advanced levels. Mine was a 10-week evening course. I went into my course thinking it would be easy. After all, I felt well-versed in listening to people and advising on solutions to their problems. However, I soon realised that counselling is not easy to do well! The key lesson I learned was that counsellors should not give advice and fix problems.

Humanistic Approach

This focuses on the individual's capacity for self-growth and self-awareness. It emphasises a person's inherent worth and ability to make positive choices. The counsellor provides a non-judgmental, empathetic environment where clients can freely explore their feelings and experiences with the belief that people are naturally inclined towards growth and self-actualisation when given the right conditions.

Check-in / Check-out

The concept of a check-in at the start of class and a check-out at the end is for the tutors and peers to get an insight into how someone is feeling and whether the course has brought up anything difficult.

Group Contract

My group of fellow trainees were invited to produce a contract that would govern how we would behave. Typical items were confidentiality, non-judgement, respect for others, etc.

Client Counselling Contract

The purpose of a client counselling contract is to establish clear expectations and boundaries for the therapeutic relationship. It outlines the roles and responsibilities of both the client and the counsellor and does some psychoeducation around the type of modality the counsellor works with. Common information to include:

- Confidentiality.
- Session structure.
- Location & time.
- Safeguarding.
- Modality.
- Fees.
- Cancellation policy.
- Complaints.

Intake

Before, or at the first session, the counsellor gathers essential information about the client such as relevant background, current issues, and goals for therapy. The intake process helps establish rapport, set expectations, and determine the appropriate therapeutic approach. Common information to include:

- Name and contact information.
- Presenting issues.
- Relevant medical information.
- Next of kin information.
- GP information.
- Outcome measuring counselling tools such as:

- Patient Health Questionnaire 9 Item Scale (PHQ-9)
- Generalised Anxiety Disorder 7 Item Scale (GAD-7)

Carl Rogers 3 Core Counselling Skills

The three core skills from Carl Rogers are central to building a good person-centred therapeutic relationship with a client.

Empathy
The counsellor's ability to deeply understand and share the feelings and experiences of the client, seeing the world through their eyes, their frame of reference. This means actively listening and trying to see things as the client sees them, without judgment.

Congruence
The counsellor's ability to ensure their words and actions align with their true feelings and beliefs. If the counsellor can show their authenticity and act consistently, this helps to create a trusting and open environment for the client to explore their difficulties.

Unconditional Positive Regard (UPR)
The counsellor's ability to accept and support a client without any conditions or judgment. This acceptance helps a client to explore their thoughts and emotions freely and fosters personal growth and self-acceptance.

REFLECTION POINT
What do you think about these core skills?
When did you last use them, or have them shown to you?

Triads

Triads are a 3-way conversation with specific roles designed to demonstrate the core counselling skills.

CLIENT: A trainee acting as the client.

COUNSELLOR: A trainee acting as the counsellor.

OBSERVER: A trainee observes the interaction and provides feedback.

You may be required to give feedback a certain way. I did 'sandwich feedback':

1. Start with something positive that worked well.
2. Followed by a learning point, something that was missed or that could have been done differently with greater effect.
3. End with something positive that worked well.

This method involves framing constructive criticism between positive comments. By starting with something positive, addressing areas for improvement, and ending with encouragement, the hope is that the other person may find it easier to accept and integrate the feedback constructively. However, I found a difficulty with the concept overall. All the trainees are being taught at the same rate, so how can the observer possibly give correct, detailed, feedback about the counsellor's efforts? The impact to me was a difficulty at times in accepting peer feedback to learn from. Tutor observations are key.

> **REFLECTION POINT**
>
> *How do you feel about doing triads?*
>
> *Which roles might you be looking forward to, or not looking forward to performing?*

Non-Verbal Communication (NVC)

Conveys empathy, understanding and support without the use of words.

- Demonstrate through body language, facial expressions, and eye contact. A counsellor can express warmth, attentiveness, and concern which helps build trust and rapport with a client.

- Observing a client's NVC allows the counsellor to gain deeper insights into their emotions and unspoken concerns.

- Consider the client's view of you – are you sitting frowning with arms crossed, or adopting an open stance with your body language looking relaxed?

Active Listening

Communication technique where the counsellor fully concentrates and understands what the client is saying, listening to understand.

- The counsellor is also paying attention to the client's tone, body language and emotions.

- Helps a client feel heard and understood.

- The counsellor can demonstrate they have listened and understood by using other counselling skills outlined below.

Reflections

The counsellor notices feelings, emotions, and content words the client has expressed, mirroring the client by repeating back exactly what was said and how.

Reflections can also clarify and validate the client's experiences, aiding in self-awareness and insight.

EXAMPLE

Client: "I just don't feel heard."

Counsellor: "Heard."

Note how the counsellor has mirrored the word 'heard' rather than repeating the word as a question, as one might be inclined to do.

Paraphrasing

The counsellor restates the client's words in a slightly different way to clarify or highlight the key points.

- The purpose is to summarise what the client has said, without changing the meaning, to help ensure the counsellor has understood the client.

- Helps the client understand their thoughts from a new perspective.

EXAMPLE

Client: "I feel overwhelmed at work. There's just too much to do and I don't know where to start."

Counsellor: "You're feeling stressed because your workload is high, and it's hard to know how to begin tackling it."

Clarifying

Statements or open questions the counsellor uses to ensure they have fully understood what the client has said.

Helps to remove ambiguity, ensuring both client and counsellor are on the same page.

EXAMPLE

Client: "I just can't deal with things anymore."

Counsellor: "When you say you can't deal with things, what specific situations or feelings are you referring to?"

Silences

Used to give clients time to reflect on their thoughts and feelings, allowing deeper emotions to surface.

- Used to create space for the client to process what has been discussed, encouraging self-exploration and insight.

- Allows the counsellor to observe the client's NVC cues and allows the client to take the lead in continuing the conversation.

- It might be useful to discuss with the client beforehand if they would be comfortable with silence, some are not.

Immediacy

Brings attention to the present moment, including the emotions, reactions, and dynamics between the counsellor and client during the session.

Allows clients to gain insights into their behaviours, patterns, and emotional responses.

EXAMPLE

Counsellor: "I've noticed that you seem a bit distant today. Can we talk about what's going on right now that might be affecting how you're feeling?"

Summarising

Used to consolidate and clarify key points of the discussion, ensuring both the counsellor and client have a shared understanding of what has been covered.

- Typically used at the end of the session to highlight to the client the main issues and themes that have come out of the session.

- Summaries may also be useful during the session to bring focus back to the client if they get a bit lost in what they have spoken about.

The course offered a good introduction to what counselling looks like. It allowed me to think about whether I wanted to pursue counselling with a negligible commitment of my time and financial resources.

Level 1 – Tick!

Top Tips

1. Consider starting a WhatsApp group or similar with the other students. This is useful to ask for help, check about assignments, provide support, and check in with each other. This will be useful throughout your training.

2. It may sound like a no-brainer but add calendar entries for when homework is due and try to stay on top of them. It is easy to underestimate the time needed to complete assignments and see those deadlines fly by in a panic. Ask tutors if they are flexible about extending deadlines.

NAILING COUNSELLING TRAINING

3. See if your tutors can recommend any counselling videos, podcasts, books, or other resources that will be useful to learn from.

4. Consider using social media to follow organisations or people that interest you. Get involved in conversations.

5. Consider volunteering for an organisation to get some practical experience. This is a good way to get involved with a community, see if you enjoy counselling, sharpen your skills and it may also help with obtaining a placement further down the line.

6. NVC can be difficult for me to show as I have a rather marvellous but unintentional Resting B Face. The more I am concentrating or interested in something, the deeper my frown gets, projecting the exact opposite of what I am thinking and feeling. When on Zoom, I find it useful to keep checking how I am appearing in the smaller pop-up window should I need to discreetly adjust my face.

7. My training started with 3-minute triads to highlight the individual core skills, increasing over time to include multiple skills over 50 minutes. A problem I encountered is that it can be challenging to ensure everyone has equal time in the counsellor role due to conversations getting side-tracked. I usually volunteered to go first, to ensure I got my time!

8. Have fun with the triads. The client's role is to support the counsellor in practising their skills, so deliver good client scenarios appropriate to the theory being covered and try out different body language to see if your counsellor notices subtleties.

9. It can be challenging not to take feedback personally or feel defensive. Remember, everyone is being taught at the same pace but the individual learning speed may differ amongst the group. Some people might not have the ability to offer constructive feedback leading to comments that may feel unhelpful or lack depth. Others might be overly kind, while some too blunt. Aim to give and receive feedback with an open mind and an objective perspective.

10. Good open question starter words are: What, When, Where, How, Describe, Tell me about, etc.

NAILING COUNSELLING TRAINING

NOTES

~ *Chapter 3* ~
Personal Awareness - Level 2

Counselling Session Structure

Counselling has a phase of three areas, a beginning, a middle and an ending. What this looks like depends on whether it is per session, or whether the phases cover several sessions. This is further complicated by whether the sessions are a set number, or open-ended.

During my training, I spent far too much time obsessively trying to figure out where the boundaries of these phases were. When did the middle part start and end?! My advice would be to just relax into the sessions. As your client talks more and more, you will pick up themes, discuss strategies, check if the strategies are working, etc, and naturally move forward. I have broken down the areas and added suggestions for what to cover in the phases.

Beginnings

At the start of counselling the focus is on building a therapeutic relationship and understanding what brings the client to therapy. The client may discuss their main concerns and set goals for what they want to achieve.

Beginning of the first session

Introduction, discuss the contract and answer questions, perform or check intake information. Discuss client goals and explore what needs to happen to reach them. This may take 10 minutes or the entire first session.

Beginning of subsequent sessions

This depends on your client. You may plan to do a brief reminder around confidentiality, or a summary of what was discussed in the previous session. However, plans go out the window if your client starts talking straight away and you cannot get a word in.

It is a good idea to remind the client how many sessions they have left (if this is known), e.g., this is session 2 of 6. This also helps remind the client that there will be an end to the sessions.

Middle

This is about the middle part of a series of sessions. As an example, if there are 12 sessions, the middle part may fall between sessions 5-9. This will depend on how your client responds to counselling. The following are some examples of what key activities might come out during this phase:

- **Deepening Exploration**: Clients delve more deeply into their issues, exploring underlying emotions, patterns, and root causes. The counsellor supports the client in understanding the complexities of their concerns and finding new, helpful ways to overcome issues.

- **Developing Insights**: Through discussion, reflection, and various therapeutic techniques, clients may gain greater self-awareness and insight into their thoughts, behaviours, and emotions.

- **Implementing Strategies**: Clients begin to apply coping strategies, skills, or interventions discussed in earlier sessions in real-life situations. Useful to start focusing the client on the end of counselling.

- **Evaluating Progress**: This is dynamic throughout all the counselling sessions. Both the counsellor and client assess if the goals are still applicable, what progress has been made towards the goals, and identify any challenges or obstacles encountered along the way. Useful to start focusing the client on the end of counselling.

Endings

Towards the end of counselling, the focus shifts to summarising the progress made and planning for the future. Both client and counsellor might review what has been learned, and how the client has grown, and discuss ways to maintain their progress after the sessions end. The goal is to ensure the client feels confident and prepared to manage challenges on their own.

Ending per session. Some suggestions:

- Awareness of time to let the client know how many minutes remain of the session, generally around 10 minutes.

- End the session, including a summary if relevant, and check the client is okay to leave.

- Confirm booking of the next session.

Ending the last session of a series of counselling sessions. Some suggestions:

Discussions about the ending should be happening before the last session so the client is aware it is coming up. The middle phase where coping strategies or change is identified is a good place to start focussing on what they can do once counselling has ended.

- **Acknowledge** the relationship between you is ending and how that feels.

- **Ask** the client how they might fill the time set aside for counselling once they have finished.

- **Review** what the client found useful during counselling, and how they will deal with any triggers once counselling has ended.

- **Discuss** any changes the client has already made or will be making.

- **Discuss** whether goals have been achieved.

- **Leave** the door open (if you are happy to!) for the client to return at a future date.

In my work now, I don't consciously think about structuring sessions with a clear beginning, middle, or end – it just happens naturally and flows.

> ### *REFLECTION POINT*
> *Have I just confused you with the different stages?*
> *How might you handle them?*

Ethical Framework

It is important to be aware of your morals and ethics as these are likely to affect your ability to work with a client.

When I was challenged to think about where mine came from, and whether they have changed over time, I realised I was not too clear on the distinction between the two.

- **Morals** – Personal belief system about what we think is right or wrong.

- **Ethics** – Principles or standards that govern the behaviour of a group or professions. Often grouped as a framework for making decisions.

> ### *REFLECTION POINT*
> *What do you understand about your morals and ethics?*
> *How might these help or impede working with clients?*

Ethical frameworks featured a lot throughout the course. Assignments and research projects were completed that considered how an ethical framework might help or hinder working with clients, and in what context, for example working in a school vs working in private practice. The two main ethical frameworks considered were the BACP and NCPS.

A client I felt I could not work with would be someone who deliberately hurt or killed another person. I just could not see myself being able to work with someone like this. I would be going into the session full of judgement and feeling anger and repulsion, so I couldn't possibly support someone who had acted in this way.

If you have had a peek at the above mentioned ethical frameworks, you will see they are huge! A counsellor needs to protect the rights, dignity, and well-being of their clients, maintain professional standards, and ensure that counselling remains a safe and supportive process. Don't panic, it is unlikely you will be expected to recite them all! You can check back with them as and when needed to ensure your understanding and actions align with your chosen framework.

Reflecting on the types of clients I felt I could and could not work with, while adhering to these frameworks, became a complex task.

Self-disclosure

Self-disclosure refers to the counsellor sharing personal experiences, feelings, or thoughts with the client.

Whether to self-disclose can be difficult to consider, especially at the moment when sitting opposite your client. Questions might run through your head about whether it is appropriate, probably as your client is talking, so you risk missing what they are saying.

If you do self-disclose, ensure that the focus remains on the client's needs and maintain professional boundaries. The goal is to support the client's growth and understanding without shifting the focus away from their issues.

I have added some examples of the impact of self-disclosure.

Pros

- Sharing relevant personal experiences might build a stronger therapeutic relationship.

- Normalises a client's experience.

- The client feels encouraged to be more open with sensitive issues.

Cons

- Shifts the focus away from the client and onto the counsellor.

- Blurs professional boundaries leaving the client overly familiar or confused about the therapeutic relationship.

- Inadvertently influences the client to share the values and perspective of the counsellor.

- The client might feel uncomfortable or less able to relate.

> ### *REFLECTION POINT*
>
> *If you have personal experience of an issue a client presents with, would you disclose this?*
>
> *How do you think self-disclosure would benefit the client?*
>
> *Are you disclosing for the client or you?*

Self-awareness

This is about understanding and reflecting on your thoughts, feelings, and behaviours and how they might impact the therapeutic process.

- It means being conscious of your personal biases, morals and ethics, and emotional triggers to recognise how these may influence your interactions with clients.

- Self-awareness helps you stay objective, manage responses, and prevent personal issues from affecting the therapeutic relationship. It's an ongoing process, even post-qualification, requiring awareness of your strengths and growth areas, which enhances your professional development and effectiveness as a counsellor.

> ### *REFLECTION POINT*
> *How self-aware do you think you are?*

NAILING COUNSELLING TRAINING

Self-care

This is about taking conscious actions to maintain your own physical, emotional, and mental well-being to effectively support your clients, seeking your own professional help if needed. Think about the type of work counsellors do, if we do not take care of ourselves, we risk burn-out.

- It includes practices such as setting boundaries to manage workload, engaging in regular supervision or peer support, and taking time for personal relaxation and hobbies.

- A peer likened self-care to being on an aeroplane when the oxygen masks drop down. You have to help yourself first before you can help others.

REFLECTION POINT

What does your self-care look like?

Do you think this might change as you experience counselling training?

The Johari Window

Created by two psychologists, Joseph Luft, and Harrington Ingham, in 1955.

The Johari Window is often used in therapy, self-help, and team-building exercises to improve communication and interpersonal relationships. The goal is to expand the **Open**

Area by sharing more about yourself (reducing the Hidden Area) and receiving feedback from others (reducing the Blind Spot). As the Open Area grows, understanding and trust in relationships also increase, leading to better communication and personal growth.

The model is typically represented as a square divided into four quadrants, each representing different aspects of self-awareness and mutual understanding between people:

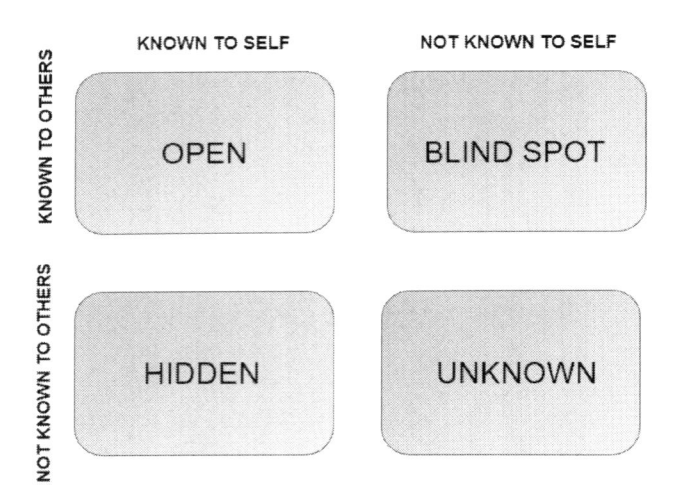

	KNOWN TO SELF	NOT KNOWN TO SELF
KNOWN TO OTHERS	OPEN	BLIND SPOT
NOT KNOWN TO OTHERS	HIDDEN	UNKNOWN

Open: Known to self and others (shared knowledge).

Blind Spot: Known to others, unknown to self (feedback area).

Hidden: Known to self, unknown to others (privacy area).

Unknown: Unknown to self and others (potential discovery area).

> **REFLECTION POINT**
> *How and why might you use this model with a client?*

Maslow's Hierarchy Of Needs

Created by Abraham Maslow, 1943. Maslow's Hierarchy of Needs is a psychological theory that outlines five levels of human needs, arranged in a pyramid structure, with basic needs at the bottom and more complex needs at the top. According to Maslow, people must satisfy lower-level needs before progressing to higher levels.

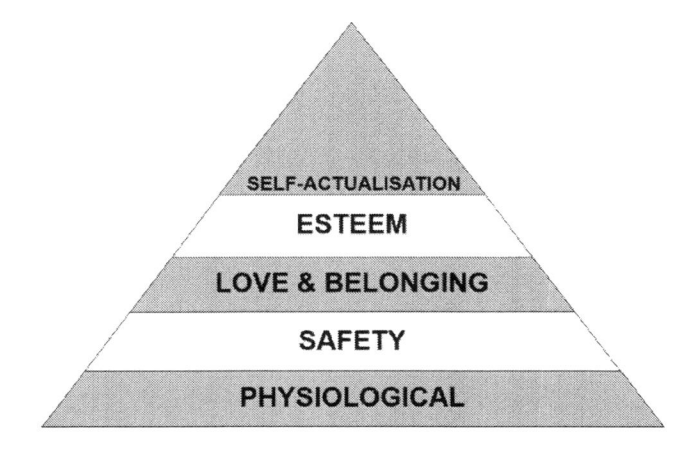

Pyramid diagram showing from top to bottom: SELF-ACTUALISATION, ESTEEM, LOVE & BELONGING, SAFETY, PHYSIOLOGICAL.

- **Physiological Needs**: These are basic survival needs, such as food, water, shelter, and sleep. They are the foundation of the hierarchy because they are essential for life.

- **Safety Needs**: Once physiological needs are met, individuals seek security and safety. This includes physical safety, financial stability, health, and protection from harm.

- **Love and Belonging**: At this level, people seek relationships, friendships, and a sense of belonging. Social connections and emotional bonds are crucial for fulfilling this need.

- **Esteem**: This involves self-esteem and the desire for recognition or respect from others. It includes achievements, confidence, and the feeling of being valued.

- **Self-Actualisation**: At the top of the pyramid is the need for personal growth and fulfilment. Self-actualisation involves realising one's full potential, pursuing creativity, and striving for personal meaning in life.

Maslow suggested that once lower-level needs are fulfilled, people naturally move up the hierarchy, but lower needs can re-emerge if unmet.

REFLECTION POINT

Do you agree with the order of Needs?

Where do you think you are on the model?

How might you use this with a client?

Research Project

I had a research project to complete which involved investigating an organisation for the placement I might do during Level 4. I picked a charity that works with children providing pre- and post-bereavement support. These are a few of the main points I had to find out about:

- How does someone get referred?
- Is there an age range?
- Is there a cost involved?
- What is the typical wait time from referral to receiving counselling?
- How is counselling received (face-to-face, telephone, video)
- Consider what limitations I might have if I secured a placement.

Although it initially felt premature to undertake this task, as I was unsure of the type of placement I wanted or what would suit me, I found it valuable to focus on some fundamental questions. This process led me to consider what counselling might look like within an organisation, and, in doing so, the reality of practising counselling began to feel more tangible to me.

Assessments

My learning throughout this level has been assessed in a variety of ways. There have been weekly journals which demonstrated a critical understanding of the various aspects of counselling learned so far, how they might be applied in different scenarios, and what the impacts might be.

The research project was marked against various criteria and was useful to see the tutor's input as to how I might prepare myself further for the placement in Level 4.

There was also a reflective element to document personal insights and progress of learning. Having tutor feedback on these, to challenge my ideas and thoughts was a good learning experience to get me thinking and reflecting even more.

Performance in all triad roles was assessed by my counselling trainee peers as well as tutor observations.

The Skills Assessment

The skills assessment was for 20 minutes with a pre-prepared scenario from the tutors. The beginning, middle and end of a session needed to be demonstrated, which is not usual for a 20-minute session!! The tutor was looking for a basic contract run-through at the beginning, identifying at least one issue and showing how this could be worked with for the middle, and that time was being managed with notice that the session was drawing to an end for the ending.

Level 2 – Tick!

Top Tips

1. It is difficult to assign the Beginning, Middle and End sections to specific session numbers. The number of sessions offered differs between counselling organisations, it might be 6, 12, 18, or open-ended sessions. A client may decide not to return so you do not get to have an ending. A client might tell you about their difficulties in the first session or spread out

over session per session or not until near the end of the allotted number of sessions if they need time to build trust. Therefore, you need to consider how you will manage this. Experience will come, keep the faith!

2. Keep a list of what type of clients you think you can and cannot work with. I found it useful at the end of training to see whether this had changed and why.

3. **Self-disclosure** - During my volunteer bereavement role, I am frequently asked by clients if I have experienced bereavement myself. I willingly say yes and usually that is enough for the client to hear. Even if the bereavement happened in similar circumstances, there are so many differences between myself and my client that it does not mean our bereavement is the same. If the client persists in wanting to find out more, then I would throw this back, e.g., "I am wondering why my experiences are important to you" and then make it all about the client again. A mini summary may be useful at this point to get the client back on track with what they were saying.

4. **Triads** - These are 30 minutes long and feel realistic at times. There is a mix of real client scenarios and made-up scenarios. The difficulty with the made-up scenarios is that you might not be able to draw out feelings and emotions too easily for your counsellor. However, the difficulty with real scenarios is to make sure that as the client you are okay with the content you are sharing, and to consider whether it is appropriate for your inexperienced counsellor to deal with.

5. **Self-care** - Even now, I still often forget to put myself first when I need to. I have to be quite disciplined about putting

boundaries in place so I have enough time for myself. Do not neglect your self-care.

6. **Johari Window** - This might be difficult to do in class with your peers to get a good idea about your self-awareness if you do not know each other well. I found it useful to do outside of training with people who know me well and are not afraid to be honest. You may find it useful to do at the beginning of your training and repeat again at the end to see if there have been changes to your Open, Blind Spot, Hidden and Unknown areas.

NOTES

~ *Chapter 4* ~
Theory Overload – Level 3

Process Group

A monthly process group was introduced to provide trainees with a safe, supportive environment to explore our interpersonal dynamics, emotions, and behaviours. In these groups, participants reflect on their experiences, give and receive feedback, and develop self-discovery and self-awareness. This setting allows trainees to understand group dynamics, improve their therapeutic skills, and gain insights into how their behaviours and feelings might influence their future clients.

In theory, this seemed like a good idea, but it wasn't a positive experience for me. The lack of structure was challenging, as conversations often strayed from the objective due to insufficient moderation. I also prefer to process things on my own and at my own pace, so I struggled with contributing to the group at a fixed time. However, recognising these preferences probably means I achieved the intended goal of self-discovery and self-awareness!

Another issue I had difficulty overcoming was one of trust. For one of the sessions over video, it appeared that one of the moderators was taking notes. I recall observing this and wondering what the reasons could be, given we were told this was a process group outside of our course tutors, was confidential and nothing would be reported back (unless a concern was raised that warranted this). I did not mention anything at the time, but this issue was brought up at a later date and no real response was ever provided. Therefore, my trust in this process was eroded and I did not contribute further. During the remaining sessions, I would think about why I had even turned up (I needed a tick for attendance), why I did not question the behaviour at the time (I did not feel empowered) and what I could have done differently (speak up!!). It was also a good reminder of how a client might feel if they ever suspect their trust has been violated.

Humanistic Models

Carl Rogers - Person-Centred Approach (PCA)
Carl Rogers, a psychologist who developed Person-Centred Therapy (PCA), which is a humanistic approach to counselling that emphasises the importance of creating a supportive, non-judgmental environment.

- The counsellor offers empathy, unconditional positive regard, and congruence, allowing clients to explore their feelings and experiences freely.

- This approach is client-led, with emphasis that the client is the expert on their life. Therefore, the counsellor facilitates self-exploration to help the client, rather than directing the client and session.

- The belief is that people have an innate capacity for self-healing and personal growth.

- There are YouTube videos that show the Carl Rogers and Gloria taped counselling that you may have heard about. Do bear in mind that these are from many years ago when attitudes were quite different to now.

Irvin Yalom - Existentialism

Irvin Yalom, a psychiatrist and psychotherapist, known for his work in existential therapy, which focuses on the fundamental human concerns of existence, such as death, freedom, isolation, and meaning.

- This approach helps clients confront and explore these existential realities, encouraging them to find personal meaning and authenticity in life despite its inherent challenges.

- Yalom's work emphasises the importance of facing the anxieties that arise from our awareness of these existential concerns and using them as a catalyst for growth, self-understanding, and deeper connections with others.

Roberto Assagioli - Psychosynthesis

Roberto Assagioli, an Italian psychiatrist founded Psychosynthesis, a therapeutic approach that integrates spiritual and psychological growth.

- This approach views individuals as more than just their psychological struggles, emphasising the development of the whole person, including their higher potential and purpose in life.

- The focus is on self-actualisation, creativity, and the exploration of a person's inner world, including the conscious and unconscious mind.

- Clients are encouraged to connect with their higher self and work towards personal growth, and the realisation of their unique potential.

Laura and Fritz Perls - Gestalt

Laura and Fritz Perls developed Gestalt therapy, a form of psychotherapy that emphasises the importance of living in the present moment and becoming aware of one's immediate thoughts, feelings, and actions.

- Focuses on helping individuals understand and integrate their experiences, promoting self-awareness and personal growth.

- Clients are encouraged to explore how they perceive and react to situations in their lives, often using role-playing and other techniques to bring unresolved issues to the surface.

- Introduces the concept of "incomplete Gestalts", where an unresolved trauma is left incomplete, referred to as "unfinished business" which can cause issues for a person if the needs are not met.

REFLECTION POINT
Do any of these Humanistic approaches resonate with you?

Non-Humanistic Models

Aaron Beck - Cognitive Behavioural Therapy (CBT)

Aaron Beck, a psychiatrist, developed Cognitive Behavioural Therapy (CBT), a widely used approach that focuses on the dynamic relationship between thoughts, feelings, and behaviours.

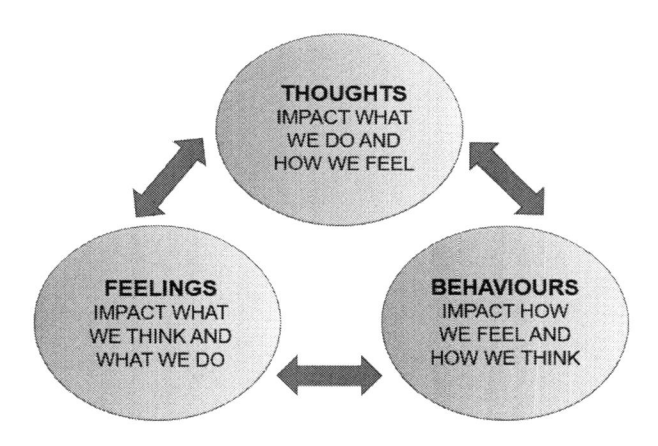

```
           THOUGHTS
        IMPACT WHAT
        WE DO AND
       HOW WE FEEL

   FEELINGS              BEHAVIOURS
  IMPACT WHAT           IMPACT HOW
  WE THINK AND          WE FEEL AND
  WHAT WE DO           HOW WE THINK
```

- The counsellor takes a directive approach, aiming to help individuals identify and challenge negative thought patterns that contribute to emotional distress and dysfunctional behaviours.

- By addressing distorted thoughts and beliefs, clients can learn to develop healthier thinking patterns and coping strategies.

- CBT is structured and goal-oriented, often involving practical exercises and problem-solving techniques to effect change.

Albert Ellis - Rational Emotive Behavioural Therapy (REBT)

Albert Ellis developed Rational Emotive Behaviour Therapy (REBT), a cognitive-behavioural approach that focuses on identifying and challenging irrational beliefs that lead to emotional distress and unproductive behaviours.

- The belief is that emotions and behaviours are largely influenced by our thoughts and beliefs *about events* rather than the events themselves.

- Clients are taught to recognise and dispute irrational beliefs, replacing them with more rational, constructive thoughts.

- Clients learn to manage their emotional responses more effectively and adopt healthier behaviours.

Activating Event – A friend passes you by and does not say hello.

Belief – I have upset them; they do not want to be friends anymore.

Consequences – I feel sad and confused, therefore I will get drunk to block them out.

Dispute – Are my thoughts factual, or driven by feelings? Does my belief match with reality? Am I jumping to the worst possible conclusion? What is the evidence for my belief?

Effect – Maybe my friend simply did not see me. When I feel sad and confused, I will talk to someone instead of drinking.

Maybe my shyness got in the way, as I could have said hello first.

Sigmund Freud – Psychodynamic

Sigmund Freud, the founder of psychoanalysis, developed the psychodynamic approach to understanding human behaviour and mental processes.

- This approach emphasises the influence of the unconscious mind, early childhood experiences, and internal conflicts on an individual's thoughts, feelings, and behaviours.

- The belief is that unresolved conflicts from childhood could manifest as psychological symptoms or maladaptive behaviours in adulthood.

- The conviction that we are controlled by our subconscious and have conflicting parts of our personality:
    - Id (uncontrolled, impulsive part of us, exists entirely in the unconscious).
    - Ego (conscious part mediating between the id and the superego).
    - Superego (judgemental and moral centre of the mind).

This therapy focuses on exploring unconscious processes through techniques such as free association, dream analysis, and examining **transference and countertransference** within the therapeutic relationship.

Transference

Clients project their feelings, attitudes, and experiences from past relationships onto the counsellor. This can involve transferring emotions and expectations related to significant figures in their lives, such as parents or authority figures, onto the counsellor.

For example, a client may respond to the counsellor as if they were a critical parent, potentially displaying childlike behaviours that influence how they engage in, and perceive the therapeutic relationship. Identifying and understanding transference can offer valuable insights into the client's unresolved issues and recurring patterns.

Countertransference

The counsellor is having a reaction to the client's transference upon them. As with the client's transference, this can involve the counsellor responding by their emotional reactions, bias, or perceptions towards their client due to unconscious feelings or issues that are brought up for the counsellor in that dynamic.

These are done at an unconscious level and may not be easily recognisable as a newbie. Even now I am qualified, I am still caught out by these at times. My supervisor alerted me to the fact that I was transferring my feelings onto one of my placement clients, even though the client was not transferring to me. This client reminded me of my younger self and I was feeling angry they were not standing up for themselves as an adult. Once I was aware of this, I was able to refocus and jump from my frame of reference back into the client's frame of reference. It took me a while to get my head around this! I find these still creep into my interactions today, they can be so subtle and sneaky!

> **REFLECTION POINT**
>
> *Have you experienced transference or countertransference?*
>
> *How do you think you might recognise them?*

Carl Jung- Analytical Psychology

Carl Jung's Analytical Psychology is a psychological framework that explores the deep layers of the unconscious mind.

- Jung introduced concepts such as the collective unconscious, which contains universal archetypes and shared human experiences, and the personal unconscious, which holds individual experiences and memories.

- Key elements of Jung's approach include the exploration of archetypes—universal symbols and themes that appear in dreams, myths, and stories, along with the journey towards integrating different aspects of the self to achieve personal growth and self-realisation.

The main archetypes used to explore the unconscious mind:

- **Persona** - a mask we might wear in certain situations if we want to come across a certain way.
- **Shadow** - our hidden or repressed self.
- **Animal/animus** - represents the feminine/masculine aspects of our psyche.

- **Self** - our balanced self.
- **Hero** - the archetype of the experiences that represent life's struggles and transformations we go through.

> ### *REFLECTION POINT*
> *Thinking about the Animal/animus, do you think this is still relevant today?*
>
> *How might you work with this?*

Donald Winnicott

Donald Winnicott, a British paediatrician, and psychoanalyst known for his influential work in child development and psychoanalysis. His work emphasises the importance of the early relationship between a child and caregiver in shaping emotional well-being and personality development.

- Introduced concepts such as the "good enough mother," which describes the importance of a caregiver's sufficient rather than perfect responsiveness to a child's needs, allowing for healthy emotional development.

- Introduced the idea of the "true self" versus the "false self," exploring how individuals develop their sense of identity through their interactions with others.

- Developed the concept of the "transitional object," such as a security blanket, which helps children manage separation and comfort during early development.

NAILING COUNSELLING TRAINING

> ### *REFLECTION POINT*
> *Does the concept of "good enough mother" resonate in other areas of life where you may strive for perfection?*

John Bowlby

John Bowlby, a British psychologist renowned for developing Attachment Theory, which explores the profound impact of early relationships on psychological development. His theory has significantly influenced our understanding of child development and the importance of nurturing relationships in forming a stable foundation for future emotional well-being.

- Bowlby proposed that the bonds formed between infants and their primary caregivers are crucial for emotional and social development.

- His work shows that a secure attachment in early childhood leads to healthier emotional and social outcomes, while insecure attachments can contribute to various psychological challenges.

He identified different attachment styles that reflect how individuals interact with others and manage relationships throughout life.

SECURE – Infants show distress upon separation from their primary caregiver. Easily comforted when the caregiver returns.

ANXIOUS – Infants show greater distress upon separation from their primary caregiver. Seeks comfort and to punish the caregiver upon their return.

AVOIDANT – Infants show minimal stress upon separation from their primary caregiver. Ignores or avoids caregiver upon their return.

DISORGANISED – Infants want a loving relationship but lash out or detach from the person giving the love. Shows inconsistent and hard-to-predict behaviour.

REFLECTION POINT

Can you identify your attachment style?

Can you see how it was formed during childhood?

How has your attachment style impacted your relationships?

Has your attachment style changed as an adult?

Schema Therapy

Schema Therapy integrates elements from other counselling approaches to address long-standing patterns of thinking, feeling, and behaving that arise from early life experiences.

- Focuses on identifying and modifying deeply ingrained schemas—persistent, negative beliefs about oneself, others, and the world, formed in childhood and carried into adulthood.

- Helps clients to understand how these schemas influence their current behaviour and relationships.

- Helps clients to challenge and reframe maladaptive schemas, develop healthier coping strategies, and build more satisfying and functional ways of interacting with themselves and others.

> ### *REFLECTION POINT*
> *Do any of these Non-Humanistic approaches resonate?*

Theory Round-up

Well, that is A LOT of theory to absorb!

They revolve around understanding thoughts, feelings, and behaviours... so how would you know which theory to pick for your client?

It will depend on what your client presents with, what their goals are, what they say in session and if they tell you what type of therapy they want.

The beauty of studying Integrative Counselling is that you get to pick and choose elements of the different models and theories.

I like the person-centred approach, and find I take inspiration from the other models and theories when needed. After gaining experience I have a sense of whether I need to bring in another approach or explore a particular theory with the client.

These areas are huge. I only went deeper with my research on topics that interested me the most. Pace yourself so you do not feel overwhelmed by it all.

It would have been interesting to cover Transactional Analysis developed by Eric Berne. I already had some awareness of this, it is useful to help clients explore their personality from the perspectives of child, adult, and parent to help support communication and interaction. I also would have liked a lot more time spent with Carl Rogers as he offers so much more besides the core counselling skills. His conditions of worth were useful in my placement. However, that is probably the nature of studying an integrative counselling course, you cannot cover everything in too much depth.

Assessments

My learning throughout this level has been assessed in a variety of ways. There have been weekly journals as per Level 2, plus some case studies to review to demonstrate a critical understanding of what counselling models might be more suited to which client scenarios and evaluate the pros and cons of this.

The research project was marked against various criteria and was a critical evaluation of how the ethical framework may help or hinder counselling that is performed in two different types of organisations.

NAILING COUNSELLING TRAINING

Performance in all triad roles was assessed by my counselling trainee peers as well as tutor observations.

The Skills Assessment

The skills assessment was for 30 minutes with a pre-prepared scenario from the tutors. The beginning, middle and end of a session needed to be demonstrated within the session, as per Level 2. There was more emphasis on the middle part for Level 3 as the counsellor needed to bring the client to a noticeably clear realisation of some kind, which would enable them to have clarity over their issues.

Level 3 – Tick!

Top Tips

1. **Gestalt** - We were not allowed to do this during our training as it requires proper Gestalt training. However, I do a couple of the techniques as part of my bereavement role and they can have quite powerful outcomes.

> *Unsent letter* – This allows the client to write to someone, saying whatever they want in whatever way they wish to express themselves, but knowing that the letter will not be sent. When I did this exercise, I found it cathartic. I attempted to burn the letter at home afterwards, but it did not catch light so I ended up drowning it! Even that felt good.
>
> *Empty chair* - This allows the client to have an imagined conversation with the empty chair, which represents the person for whom they have unsaid words.

2. **Process Group** – Try to approach this with an open mind. It is a good time to practise your active listening skills and see what reactions come up for you. This might not be to your liking, but try to be patient and speak out if you do not understand what it is all about. I wish I had given this a second chance instead of shutting down. A point to bear in mind is that this is not a counselling session, so watch any 'rescuing' tendencies you might have.

3. **Weekly journal assignment** - Now a lot of theory has been covered, my course criteria for the assignment homework is integrating the core skills with the theory, different approaches, as well as the different stages of counselling (beginning, middle, ending). It is hard work but gets you thinking. It is worth thinking about how you might use the skills in the different approaches, what might or might not work and why. There is also more personal reflection required, so keep up the work on reflecting on how something you learn might resonate with you.

4. **External course buddy for triads** - A post from a counselling Facebook page I had followed asked if anyone was interested in creating a triad group to demonstrate skills. I thought this sounded interesting and I wanted to use my skills on people outside of my counselling trainee group as it was feeling a bit too comfortable and familiar. I reached out to this person and we agreed to try some triads over Zoom. We ended up having quite a few triads and giving each other feedback which I found quite valuable coming from someone who was doing a different counselling course to me but at the same level. This experience also helped with confidence for my assessment, which is what I was hoping for.

NAILING COUNSELLING TRAINING

5. **Thinking About Placement** – See if your course provider can advise on when it might be best to start looking. They may be able to help or recommend placements that previous students went to. If you are doing volunteer work, they may be able to accept you as a student on placement. Make sure you know how many face-to-face hours you will need, and whether the sessions need to be recorded. Consider if you need to get a CV and cover letter produced. I had to convert a CV with 25+ years of testing software and hardware into one that drew out the counselling skills, so I gave focus to areas of my work that were counselling-friendly and used counselling terminology. If there is a specific advert you are replying to you can tailor your CV to that.

NOTES

~ *Chapter 5* ~
The Final Year – Level 4

Children & Young People (CYP)

Understanding the differences between working with CYP and adults allows counsellors to provide age-appropriate support, create a trusting therapeutic relationship, and ensure the well-being of the child or young person.

Discussions centred around ethical considerations in counselling related to the cognitive, social, physical, and emotional development of children and young people. Additionally, to consider were intersectional factors—such as socioeconomic status, religion, race, and gender—and how these can influence child development.

Understanding the differences between counselling CYP and adults is important for several reasons:

- **Developmental Stages**: Children and young people are at different cognitive, emotional, and social developmental stages compared to adults. Counsellors need to tailor their approach based on the client's developmental level to ensure the interventions are appropriate and effective.

- **Communication Styles**: Children often express themselves through play, art, or behaviour, while adults may articulate their thoughts verbally. Understanding these differences helps counsellors choose the right tools and methods to engage the client.

- **Emotional Regulation**: Children and young people may struggle with identifying and regulating emotions due to their developmental stage. Counsellors must be skilled in helping them recognise feelings and develop coping mechanisms, often using more creative or indirect methods than with adults.

- **Family and Environmental Influence**: Children and young people are heavily influenced by their family, school, and social environments. Counselling may involve addressing family dynamics, peer relationships, or external factors that might not be as prominent in adult counselling.

- **Confidentiality and Boundaries**: Confidentiality can be more complex with younger clients, as counsellors may need to involve parents or guardians in certain situations, such as safeguarding concerns. Balancing the child's understanding of counselling and getting their agreement, as well as a need for privacy with legal and ethical responsibilities is crucial.

- **Different Therapeutic Goals**: The goals of counselling may vary between children and adults. With children, the focus might be on behavioural or emotional regulation, while adults may seek to address long-standing personal issues or trauma.

REFLECTION POINT
How might you work differently with children and adults?

Differences And Diversity

The classroom discussions centred around emphasising the importance of recognising when someone differs from us, touching on key areas such as ethnic origin, religion, colour, gender, sexuality, sex, disability, and socioeconomic status.

Some reasons why differences and diversity matters:

- **Building Trust and Rapport**: When counsellors acknowledge and respect the diverse identities of their clients, it promotes a sense of trust and safety. Clients are more likely to open up when they feel their unique experiences are understood and valued.

- **Tailoring Interventions**: Understanding a client's cultural, social, and personal background allows counsellors to tailor their interventions more effectively. What works for one person may not work for another due to differences in beliefs, values, and life experiences.

- **Avoiding Bias and Assumptions**: Being aware of diversity helps counsellors recognise and challenge their own biases and assumptions. This awareness prevents misunderstandings and ensures that the counselling process is fair and unbiased.

- **Supporting Client Identity and Empowerment**: For clients who belong to marginalised or under-represented groups, having their identity acknowledged and respected can be empowering. It reinforces their sense of self-worth and can be a crucial part of their healing and growth.

- **Addressing Systemic Issues**: Many clients face challenges related to systemic discrimination and inequality. A counsellor who is attuned to diversity issues can help clients navigate these challenges and advocate for their rights, both within and outside the therapeutic setting.

> **REFLECTION POINT**
> *How might you work with difference and diversity with your clients?*

Ethics And Morals Revisited

Regularly reviewing ethics and morals in counselling is important to ensure client protection, professional integrity, and the counsellor's continuous development.

- **Ensures Client Safety and Well-being**: Regularly reviewing ethical guidelines helps counsellors prioritise the safety and well-being of clients, ensuring they are protected from harm, exploitation, or misconduct.

- **Guided decision-making in Complex Situations**: Ethical reviews help counsellors navigate difficult situations, such as managing relationships, confidentiality issues, or conflicts of interest. This reflection strengthens the counsellor's ability to act appropriately in challenging scenarios.

- **Promotes Accountability**: Continuous ethical reflection holds counsellors accountable to their clients, their profession, and society. It reinforces the importance of being transparent, honest, and responsible in their actions.

- **Prevents Burnout and Boundary Violations**: Regularly revisiting ethical and moral principles encourages counsellors to reflect on their boundaries and self-care practices, reducing the risk of burnout or boundary violations that could negatively affect their clients.

- **Supports Professional Growth**: Ethical reviews promote ongoing learning and self-awareness. They allow counsellors to identify areas for growth, understand evolving ethical standards, and stay aligned with the values of the counselling profession.

Based on the learning and experience obtained since Level 2, how have my morals changed? They have not changed as such, they now have greater depth. I stated I could not work with someone who deliberately hurt others, but now I would be open to trying. I would be curious about the person's background and motivation for their actions and whether I would be able to offer them support to enable healthier thoughts, feelings, and behaviours.

REFLECTION POINT
Have your ethics or morals changed since thinking about these at an earlier level?

Class Placement Supervision

A monthly group supervision was provided by the training organisation where the time could be counted towards the required monthly placement supervision hours.

NAILING COUNSELLING TRAINING

At my first training organisation-led supervision session, I was interrupted within the first 5 minutes by the 'supervisor' as I was describing a client interaction and told – while laughing - that I *"**do not have the ability to do this job.**"*

This professionally qualified person, who I was later to discover was not a qualified supervisor, did not even show basic counselling skills in listening or clarification at a minimum. I was stunned into silence and just stared at them. Two of my peers in the same supervision group just stared at me while a third peer laughed along. I was in a state of utter shock, unable to say anything. I had experienced the freeze/fight/flight state.

It was an appalling experience, but I did not let these comments knock my confidence. I know I do have the ability to do this job. My experience with my placement clients and externally qualified supervisor demonstrated to me that I can do this job.

Maybe this person is hearing something from me that I am not aware of that leads them to say this. Nonetheless, after being interrupted within 5 minutes of speaking and with zilch constructive feedback to justify that comment, I dismissed this person as unprofessional and unethical in my mind. This interaction affected the remaining class placement supervision sessions with this person and my peers. Harm had been done. I no longer had trust or faith in this process and felt a need to protect myself and my clients, so I barely contributed to further sessions with this person. At this point, I queried whether to remain on the course as this was another example where trust had been destroyed, but I was already well into Level 4, and the end was so close, so I remained. Thankfully, a qualified supervisor was brought in to replace this person for the remaining sessions, who managed to restore my faith. I also had a wonderful external supervisor who helped me gain confidence and complete the placement.

This incident gave me a good reminder to bear in mind with my clients, that sometimes we do not react at the moment in ways that we wish we did in retrospect. When I think back to it now, I wish I had challenged that statement and been able to have a reasoned discussion on what my perceived failings were. Lesson to learn, do not be afraid to challenge tutors or supervisors and lodge a complaint if you consider there to be inappropriate conduct.

REFLECTION POINT

If you encounter something similar, how might you react?

Assessments

Case Study

I needed to complete a case study that was 7500 words, broken down with specific criteria based on one placement client.

I found it easier to think about each of my clients against the criteria and started jotting down notes to see which client was starting to give me the most criteria coverage. The case study emphasis was critical analysis, critical analysis, and more critical analysis! Anytime I felt I had something solid I could use for specific criteria; I would write this up so the case study was very much a work in progress rather than try to complete it all in one go.

Course Work Assessments

Assessments for Level 4 are a mix of reflective journals, numerous presentations, peer and tutor observations, the case study on a placement client, a 50-minute skills assessment, one hundred supervised placement hours, and supervisor and placement manager reports.

The Final Skills Assessment

The tutor supplied the scenarios the day before our assessment. The assessment was a recorded 50-minute face-to-face humanistic session, showing a beginning, middle and end. Timewise, the minimum session time allowed was 48 minutes, the maximum was 52 minutes. Timings outside of these were a failure.

The assessment itself was okay. I relaxed and simply thought of it as if a real client were sitting opposite me, as per my placement experience. I had some picture cards with me and used these during the middle part as an aide for the client to visualise their issue and possible solutions.

Level 4 – Tick!

Top Tips

1. **Class supervision -** If your training organisation provides this (many do not), it will be worth asking questions up front, such as is the person a qualified supervisor. What supervision modality did they train in? How long have they been a supervisor? Do they have experience with the type of clients you are seeing on your placement? Are you able to change

supervisor if you do not get on with the initially allocated supervisor?

2. **Case Study** - I started making notes on the various criteria from my first client, usually after I had written up session notes. It can be easy to leave this and think there is enough time to do this later, but while the information was fresh in my head, I wanted to get it down so I did not forget anything and could capture emotion and feelings. It is worth thinking about when to submit your case study if you are looking to have submitted all your coursework by a certain date. Find out how long it roughly takes for the external marker to return work. Also, if you fail the case study, find out if you need to re-write the entire case study or just those sections that scored lower marks.

3. **The Final Assessment** - If you can, relax. I found this assessment easier/less stressful than the Level 3 assessment. My placement experience helped as I was gaining skills and confidence, so I just went into it imagining this was a real session.

NOTES

~ Chapter 6 ~
Personal Counselling

NAILING COUNSELLING TRAINING

My course required me to complete 10 hours of personal counselling from the start of Level 3 and complete it by the end of Level 4. This is an additional cost to bear in mind.

When choosing a counsellor, I had two specific criteria in mind. Firstly, since my peer group and tutors were all women, I wanted to work with a non-female counsellor to gain a different perspective. Secondly, although my course provider offered a counselling service, I preferred to find someone external to experience a fresh approach. I was also comfortable with video sessions, which allowed me to attend counselling from the convenience and comfort of home.

I was looking for someone to help me with an eating disorder, as I can't shake the worry that potential clients might judge me as unfit if it seems like I haven't dealt with my eating struggles. When I came across brief biographies of two counsellors specialising in eating disorders, I immediately dismissed one based solely on their photo, which showed them as quite large. I realised I had just judged someone I do not know, based on a picture that might be outdated—exactly the kind of judgment I feared others will pass on me. I do not feel good about this, but I still find myself questioning how this person could help me if they (seemingly) haven't overcome their eating issues. Oddly enough, if I were seeking counselling for a different issue, I would have no reservations about working with them.

After a brief search, I found someone who seemed like a good fit—a male counsellor who offered student discounts, one-hour sessions, and the option for video counselling. I reached out, and we had an initial conversation where he got to know more about my concerns, and I learned about his therapeutic approach. The conversation went well, and we scheduled my first session. While I am committed to fully engaging as a client to make the most of this experience, I am also keen to observe how he interacts with me as part of my learning process.

As I usually find with my bereavement volunteer work, the first session is a data dump from the client, which I had no trouble doing at all! It feels like I am talking non-stop. This surprises me as I do not think I have much to say, as generally, I am a listener, not a talker. I like to give and receive information linearly, but I am jumping all over the place as I remember different things I consider important.

I had never opened up about my issues to anyone before, and it felt incredible to finally share them with someone who listened intently, showing genuine empathy and interest. Throughout the first session, I noticed my counsellor using paraphrasing, asking clarifying questions, and posing open-ended questions to find out more. Towards the end, he offered some reflections that he hadn't mentioned earlier, explaining that they could be quite powerful and worth exploring further in future sessions. I was impressed by how well he understood and accurately reflected what I was expressing. I felt I could speak honestly with him, without feeling judged. This was a refreshing contrast to past experiences with doctors or nurses (who might be overweight themselves!) simply telling me to eat less and move more. If it were that simple, I would have done it by now! Sometimes, psychological support is essential to uncover the underlying reasons behind our behaviours.

My challenge is that eating is a fundamental part of life, making it nearly impossible not to think about. Several times a day I am confronted with food—whether it's deciding what meals to have or choosing what to buy when shopping. There is no avoiding the topic of food.

I am usually a private person, but I found myself able to open up to a stranger. He demonstrated such strong counselling skills—even over video—that I felt comfortable sharing, and once I started, I did not want the session to end. Afterwards, it truly felt like a weight had been lifted.

The next couple of sessions were a further exploration of my issues. I am asked to rate from 0 – 10 (with 10 being high) what I consider my self-worth is, how much I like myself and what I think others might say about this. This introduces some Carl Rogers' concepts:

External Locus of Evaluation - The tendency to rely on others' opinions, judgments, and expectations to determine one's self-worth, decisions, and behaviour. When someone has an external locus of evaluation, they are guided by external validation rather than trusting their own feelings, values, and judgments.

Internal Locus of Evaluation - A person looks inwards for self-assessment, relying on their thoughts and feelings to guide their decisions and sense of self-worth. Developing an internal locus of evaluation is essential for personal growth, self-acceptance, and living an authentic life.

Conditions of Worth – The expectations or standards imposed by others (like parents, peers, or society) that a person feels they must meet to gain approval, love, or acceptance. When people internalise these conditions, they may suppress their true feelings or desires and behave in ways that align with others' expectations, even if it goes against their authentic self.

Further sessions became super interesting as my counsellor had managed to get me thinking about when the issues started and how they changed over time to cope with various things I went through as I got older. For instance, I was bullied at school from the ages of 11-16 years by some peers and people 2 years older than me. This is a crucial time for cognitive development of thinking, reasoning, problem-solving, building confidence, and forming relationships as part of puberty. Counselling has allowed me to consider how the bullying and my subsequent coping mechanisms have affected me throughout life.

With my self-confidence and self-esteem at an all-time low, I carried the same behaviours from school into every job I had. It was time to be honest with myself: while some people are indeed unpleasant or incompetent, affecting my ability to do my best work, I had been playing the victim for too long. I blamed others for my unhappiness and turned to food to reinforce my unhealthy habits. I realised I needed to take responsibility and change my reactions, because, as an adult, they were no longer serving me well.

I reached these conclusions thanks to the thought-provoking insights and questions posed by my counsellor as he gave me those three core skills in our sessions. He accomplished something truly powerful for me in a short amount of time. When he asked what I felt I had missed out on in life, well, that opened up another can of worms!

I cannot thank my counsellor enough for being by my side as I opened up and reflected on the underlying causes of my issues with food. The hard work is ongoing as I adopt more healthier reactions, and I am open to receiving further support for this battle if I feel I need it. I recommend everyone should have some form of counselling at least once in their lives, and do not be surprised if it leads you to unexpected places.

NOTES

~ *Chapter 7* ~
100 Hour Placement – Level 4

One of the most exhilarating yet nerve-wracking aspects of counselling training is the placement experience. For me, it was both the most dreaded and the most exciting part of the journey. The moment I was cleared by my training organisation and finally secured a placement, I was overwhelmed with a euphoric mix of pride, relief, and anticipation. But those emotions didn't stop there. The first hour felt so nerve-wracking—I was stiff, anxious, and questioning everything. Fast forward to my 100th hour, and I was a completely different person. Not wanting the session to end, I felt relaxed and was fully immersed in the growth and connection with my clients that had developed along the way. The transformation was a rollercoaster, but an unforgettable one!

Detailed here are the situations I encountered, things I did not get right, and how a newbie dealt with it all.

This is a good section to reflect on what you might do if faced with similar.

Preparing For Placement

1. Figure out what type of placement and clients you want experience of working with. It can be tempting to just take anything offered, but question if you can give 100%, and what you are taking away from the experience if it does not tick all your boxes.

2. Find out if your course provider helps students find placements or is prepared to say where previous students undertook their placements.

3. Try GP surgeries, nursing homes, hospices, and prisons.

4. Try schools/colleges/universities – useful to find out the safeguarding lead and speak to them.

5. I googled organisations that offered counselling and then contacted them to see if they accept student placements.

6. If you are volunteering in a counselling-related organisation, can they take you on?

7. Make sure you have your "fitness to practise" sign-off from your tutor.

Find Out About Your Placement

1. Check they have a Safeguarding policy, including adults, children, and vulnerable people.

2. Who is around for you to go to, is it in person or by phone, what times is the safeguarding lead available, and who else can cover if the main person is unavailable?

3. When to break confidentiality and how.

4. Health & Safety policy.

5. First aid policy.

6. Fire Procedure.

7. Lone worker policy.

8. GDPR policy.

9. Gifts/renumeration policy.

10. Complaints procedure.

11. Can you work with adoption-related issues?

12. What is the admin overhead like?

13. Are they willing to sign off on your counselling organisation's placement paperwork?

14. Note taking – any particular format, how are they stored, how long are they kept for?

15. Is student membership in a counselling organisation required.

16. Do you need a Disclosure and Barring Service (DBS), or Enhanced DBS? If you do not have one, can the placement arrange this for you? If you do obtain one, get it on the Update Service (this allows other organisations to view your certificate without necessarily having to get a separate DBS per organisation).

17. Does the placement provide insurance? If not, you will need student insurance (make sure you are covered for Professional Indemnity and Public Liability and anything else needed). If you do get your own placement insurance, check the terms as it may differ from your placement, especially regarding note keeping.

18. Do they offer supervision and is it free?

19. If you have supervision from outside your placement, do you have permission to talk (anonymously) about your clients? Some organisations do not allow this, so do check.

20. Some course providers require students to video the sessions. Check if this is okay with the placement AND the clients.

21. Can they give you a tour and meet people before you start?

22. I have yet to know of anyone getting paid for their placement, but check if travel expenses are reimbursed, and any other perks you may be offered.

Social Media Presence

Before you start with clients, review your private social media privacy settings. If you upload family pictures, are these private or can anyone see them?

A client might want to find out more about you, or even request you add them as a friend or professional connection.

My Placement

I needed to find a placement that offered a minimum of 51 hours face-to-face. The remaining hours could be conducted over video or telephone calls.

I fired off thirty-seven applications for placements, a mix of speculative and applying for advertised placement opportunities. A couple of websites I looked at required a fee to even look at an application, which would only be refunded if the applicant was successful. I gave those a hard pass. Most applications were not replied to. Some placements require a deposit, and you have to agree to sign up for a minimum time frame or forfeit the deposit. Again, I gave those a pass.

I managed to secure a wonderful placement. I would be seeing clients from age 13 to 26 years, with a range of issues, a tier two charity (mental health services provided by professionals, e.g. counsellors), I could do evenings after work and more importantly, it was face-to-face. To top it off, two other peers on my course also gained placements at the same charity. Perfect! I started in August, just before the start of Level 4.

Counselling Intake

My placement manager performed the intake and would provide me with the information so I could decide if I wanted to accept the client. I found that clients do not always want to disclose reasons why they would like some counselling at the intake stage. This certainly led to some surprises along the way and discussions around whether I was the best person to be providing counselling.

Early on I was faced with a client involved in an ongoing police investigation that was not mentioned at intake. I did a lot of research on the implications of this and spoke to my placement manager and supervisor. I had to prepare for potentially going to court, or at least need to submit my counselling notes. Would this change how I performed the counselling? How should I write my notes if I write them at all in this case? I reminded my client about reasons for breaching confidentiality, and that a judge may compel me to submit my notes. I explained how I was going to take notes (very factual and brief) and offered to show the notes to my client at each session, so nothing was a surprise. The client did not come back for further sessions.

Be prepared that what information you have at intake, may not be what you end up talking about!

Contracting

I followed the placement's contracting; it was fairly standard:

- Confidentiality and when this may be breached.
- Safeguarding.
- Number of appointments, time, duration, and frequency.
- Notice period to rearrange or cancel appointments.
- Circumstances when appointments would be cancelled by the charity.
- GDPR, note taking and storage.
- Contact methods.
- COVID-19 policy.
- Details of my membership body and Code of Conduct.

I added additional things over time, such as if the client is late (depending on if child or adult), would they want me to call them? Are they currently receiving counselling elsewhere? What is their understanding of counselling? What are their goals? And some psychoeducation around how I work.

After this stage had been completed, with no further questions, I would invite the client to start. I usually said something like "What brings you to counselling?", "What's been going on?", "I see you have provided some information at intake; I would like to hear from you what has been going on", or "If you're feeling comfortable, would you like to make a start?". These were pretty much my starting points, depending on the client's age and how they seemed up to that point.

Safeguarding

Before going into placement, you should be clear from your course training and placement policy on what safeguarding is, how to work with it, and how to break confidentiality.

Whilst I was made aware of safeguarding during training, this was not experienced during the course either via triad practise or how to have 'The Conversation' with a client if you suspect a safeguarding issue. Luckily, I had a more comprehensive understanding from my bereavement volunteer role, but I felt a little unprepared going into my placement.

As a trainee on placement, I took every concern I had to my placement manager and my supervisor. This included self-harming where a client was excessively scratching themselves causing marks, as I did not want to risk missing anything. I felt such a responsibility to get this right, so it was a great learning experience to be supported by both my placement manager and supervisor.

When contracting with a client, it should be stated clearly what safeguarding is, your obligations and your client's agreement that they understand this. This message can always be repeated at other sessions if you feel it is necessary.

NAILING COUNSELLING TRAINING

Breaking Confidentiality
Sitting across from someone who confides that they hurt themselves and/or do not want to be here anymore needs careful management, as I am sure you know or can imagine. Language needs to be explicit to ensure you clearly understand what your client is saying, and what you are saying back to your client.

Whilst breaking confidentiality is explained at the first session when I go over the contract, I would also remind the client in the session if I was concerned about them based on what they had disclosed. I knew I would be seeking advice from my placement manager in the first instance, so I would explain my reasons to the client. I would also update my client on the outcome of the conversation with my placement manager.

Something important to consider about your placement is where are you going to be, for instance, the next day if you have raised a concern with your placement. If you are carrying clients in your head, are you going to be okay to work? If you need to call your placement manager or vice versa, can you take the call in work in a confidential space?

This situation did not enter my head before going into placement. There were plenty of times I struggled to focus on work and had to leave the lab to have a confidential conversation about safeguarding.

Safety Plan/Box
After seeing a client with an extremely low mood who did not want to be here anymore, we created what they called a "hope box." This was an old shoe box of theirs which they decorated and then filled with things that made them feel good. These

were items related to the senses, so something visual, something with a comforting smell, their favourite music, a favourite snack, or a drink. They also included pictures they liked to look at, pens, paper and colouring books, reading books and wrote some things down they like to do such as pet the dog or watch TV on pieces of paper and would randomly pick one of these to do. The idea is that when the low mood struck, they could choose to go to the hope box and immediately be faced with all the things that gave them feel-good feelings. I also added phone numbers of local and national organisations that provided a listening ear – be sure to add opening times if not a 24/7 service.

Attempted Suicide
I had one young client who attempted to end their life. They said it was the safeguarding element of where I may have to break confidentiality that stopped them from telling me. To say the bottom dropped out of my world at that moment is an understatement. As there had been an escalation in the client's behaviour, I informed my placement manager, and our sessions stopped. They were referred to a specialist service.

Self-Harming
I had a few young people who self-harmed where their parents did not know. If the situation were not serious enough to be a safeguarding issue, my placement manager and supervisor advised this is not something I would need to disclose to their parents. I felt guilty about that and would frequently take to supervision to work through.

Conversely, sometimes the level of input needed is to ensure the client is aware of wound hygiene. If they are cutting, is the implement sterilised? If they draw blood, do they know how to clean the wound to prevent infection?

Safeguarding Others
I once missed a potential safeguarding issue which was not an immediate threat to my client. It was only when I was writing my notes up the next morning, I realised I had information that suggested not only had my young client experienced (in my opinion) an inappropriate interaction, but their much younger sibling had also, and I needed to safeguard them too.

During the session I had noted to myself that I would seek advice on the situation the next day as there was no imminent need at the time, but why had I not twigged there was another person also impacted? I took this to supervision.

Awareness Of Time

Although I had a clock in the room, it was in an awkward space on the wall above the door. To look at it I would need to keep turning my head. I bought an analogue clock, as I wanted to see the complete clock face, and made sure as best I could with the reviews that it was not a noisy ticking clock. Having time ticking by loudly was not what I wanted. I could have used my phone, and I did for the first session as I had not thought to bring a clock. However, I was soon distracted by message notifications (it was on silent) and then it went into sleep mode as it was not used for a few minutes, so managing the time was more stressful on that occasion.

Going forward, I would position the clock on the table that was to the side of my client and I, roughly in the middle so we could both see it, but turned more towards me so I could discreetly eyeball that big hand.

First Client, First Hour

I started with a client a couple of months after being offered the placement, just before the start of Level 4. I was incredibly nervous. I am a middle-aged white woman, and I was seeing a young man, what would he think of me? Do I say I am a trainee? The charity website states some counsellors are working towards the end of their qualification and are trainees.

There was not much information on the intake, and I spent an inordinate amount of time scrutinising every word, my brain firing off in all directions about what they might say and how I might respond. It feels like I covered every scenario in my mind.

I had the contract and forms to fill in laid out and ready in the room I was given to use, arranged chairs, got out the box of tissues, and checked the clock was showing the correct time and was working. I chose not to provide water, as figured this could become expensive after one hundred hours if my clients got used to it. It is only 50 minutes; they can bring their own. I did keep a small bottle of water out of sight in my bag in case of some kind of emergency, excessive coughing, choking or if someone got very upset, but I never needed to use it. I then sat quietly in the room for about half an hour before they were due, feeling a mix of calmness and panic. I sat in both chairs as I was not sure which chair the client would pick, and looked around at the view from both chairs, adjusting blinds to keep out the sun and making final little tweaks until it was time to collect my client.

When we got into the room, my client sat down, and I stood up ready to go through the paperwork. Nooooo!!! my mind screamed. Power imbalance, I am towering over him! The chairs were quite heavy, and I made a clumsy first attempt to discreetly drag mine over to where he was, but I could not shift the chair so had to carry it over. My attempt to look experienced, cool, and collected was destroyed. I do not think he noticed in the slightest. But note to self, for all future first sessions I made sure both chairs were near the table with the paperwork, and I would then just push mine back into position when we were ready to begin the session.

Invite The Client To Start
After the contracting and other paperwork were completed and signed, with no further questions at that point, I invited my client to start. I had nothing to fear. My first client was engaged, speaking almost non-stop. My active listening skills were well and truly put to the test. I gave a warning the end of the session was approaching, and my client reported (unprompted) feeling better just having someone to listen to them. I gave a summary and confirmed our next session. Phew, I took a breath.

Being Door Knobbed
At the end of the first session, I was what is known in the counselling industry as 'door knobbed.' This is a last-minute communication from the client where they are attempting to deliver important information with their hand (physically or metaphorically) on the doorknob as we exit the room.

My client said they would tell me something at the next session they had not told anyone else. What do you do with that as you are both walking out?! I muttered something like "Okay."

I mentioned this at supervision. I wanted to know how I should have handled that. A tip – you could say something like "Interestingly, this has come up at the end of our session. If you would like, we can discuss this at our next session." Also, my supervisor explored with me how I felt having that dropped on me at the end of the session. Have I been thinking about what the information might be? I might not ever get to find out what that information was if the client does not reference it again, so how would I feel about that?

It was not referenced again, so I will never know.

One Hour Down!
Once that first session was over, I was on a major high. I had done it. The first session with the first client went well. Tick! It felt a little strange not having an observer give me feedback. I was bursting, I wanted to talk about it there and then, but had to wait for my next supervision session so I could tell all.

That 10 Minute Warning

In triad practise in class, it seemed easy to signal the session was coming to an end. The person in the client role was very well behaved and knew this would be coming up so played along.

With my placement clients, I found it a little more challenging. The session was real, with real issues, and emotions were not far from the surface. In my early days, some sessions did overrun by a few minutes as I was finding my way to manage this in a more time effective way. However, as time went on, my growing experience and confidence usually meant I was able to manage the warning okay. If a client was upset at the end, or the session had been emotional for them, I would bring the session to a close, acknowledging their feelings. This might mean doing some breathing exercises together for calmness, or gently change the focus to any evening or weekend plans, or enquire about an interest or hobby they may have previously mentioned to shift the mood. I would be mindful if I knew they were driving and suggest they continue with some deep breathing before they drive off.

For some clients I found it hard to get a word in. A peer shared a suggestion they were told, which is to wait for an appropriate moment - you have to be quick here if they are a talker - and simply say, "And breathe". These two simple words allowed the client to pause and catch their breath, and for me to take a little control if I felt I needed to ask questions or comment on what had been said. Otherwise, I would let the client talk. I found that a really handy tip, and interrupts the other person without being rude.

Are you sitting comfortably?

At some point well into my placement, I became aware that I was being a German Shepherd. Short story – I have adored this breed of dog since childhood and am desperate to have a few. Therefore, when cute videos of them appear on my social media feeds I usually watch them. I noticed that there are a lot of videos of them moving their heads from side to side. One day, as I was sitting with a client, I suddenly became aware that I had tilted my head to the side, almost ninety degrees! I slowly corrected the head tilt and then overcompensated by going almost 90 degrees the other way!

Now I am ultra-conscious of my head tilting and realise I do this a lot. I wonder how it must look from the client's perspective. Does it look like I am listening and concentrating on them? Does it look like I might be bored? Does it annoy them? I guess I do not look as cute as a German Shepherd does.

Communication Mediums

During intake, the placement manager would arrange the date and time of the first session. After that, it was for me to manage directly with the client. I initially created an email address and used this for communication and later on I bought a cheap smartphone. I managed to lose the phone a short time after, but it made no difference as email was fine with my clients.

If you decide to use your personal phone, make sure to withhold the number.

Before you start spending money on a second phone and sim deal, it might be worth waiting to see if you need it.

What Is The Client's Idea Of Counselling?

During the first session with a client, I would ask what goals the client would like to be working towards or have met. That question then led some clients to confess they did not know what counselling was about. That left me a tad baffled, as why seek out counselling if you do not know much about it? I then included the question "What is your understanding of counselling?" And "How would you like counselling to support you?" I was surprised to learn that some of the young people only had American TV shows as a reference for what counselling is. They thought they might lie down while I took notes. I would do some psychoeducation and explain what counselling is and how I work. The client needs to input, so they need to be able to convey information in some form or other, and how we might work with that.

Client Notes

My placement did not have any applications or systems I needed to upload the notes to. I was responsible for writing them how I wished and storing them securely.

I handwrote my client notes and kept them factual and brief, recording key points that seemed to dominate the session. I used client initials as an identifier. I would store these at home in a locked fireproof cabinet when I was not in session with the client.

I added calendar entries when the time frame was up for storing client notes as a reminder to securely shred them.

Working With Multiple Clients

All I can say here is to manage your diary well. I recall taking on two clients at the same time early on in my volunteer role. I was petrified I would call the wrong client or get their name and notes mixed up.

Fast-forward towards the end of my placement, I had six clients per week. Due to the level of client no-shows, I averaged four clients per week. Not once did I mix their names or notes up. It worked well when adding their appointments to my diary and phone to also note the session number, so I did not have to rely on my notes for this information and was useful when making the next appointment.

That's Rude!

One client was rude from the offset. As I read the contract, they grabbed the pen, signed the form, and almost threw it at me while yawning and rolling their eyes. I sat there feeling a mixture of amusement and panic. This is new for me! It was important I remained calm and did not show on the outside what I was feeling in the inside. I did not want to rise to their bait. I looked at them, thanked them for signing the form, and said that it is important I read this out, so I will continue. They remained seated but crossed their arms with a "hmph" sound and a further eye roll.

That communication told me a lot about that client. Probably no trust in the counselling process that they may not have even understood, an issue with authority if that was how I was perceived, and that was the way they communicated with me to tell me exactly how they felt. I could not help but wonder what hurt or pain was behind this display of bravado. That is why I managed to keep calm, and gently but determinedly finish reading the contract. After I had finished I asked if they had any questions and were still happy to have signed the contract. I saw this client for quite a few sessions, the later ones did not show quite this level of behaviour. Over time they stopped acting like this, started to talk and showed a curiosity about what counselling is.

I was surprised at how I acted in the moment. With this job, you do not get to know how someone will act or what they will say, so there is no time to think things through or have a rehearsal. In my personal life I would not entertain anyone who acted like that and realised in that moment I had choices. I could have ended before we began, I could have reacted similarly or stopped speaking and bowed to them. But I hope I chose the better reaction, one that was appropriate to the reasons why I wanted to be a counsellor, which is to be curious, listen, and show those beautiful skills of empathy, congruence, and UPR to my client.

Being Late For Your Client

On the way to placement one day the road ahead had been closed. I started to panic. The only other route I knew was a long way around which meant I might just make it in time. As I joined many other cars that had also turned around, I realised that I would be unable to contact the client directly whilst driving (I had a hands-free setup). My client's paperwork with their contact details was in the boot of my car and there was nowhere to pull over safely. Panic set in. Luckily, I made it with 15 minutes to spare. Have a plan for if you might be late!

The Client Needs To Engage In Counselling

Some of the young people I saw did not necessarily have the idea themselves that they wanted to come to counselling. It was the school or parent that felt counselling might be beneficial and the young person agreed to try it. Except in one case. I had met a new client, a young person. We went through to the room where we did the contracting and other paperwork and then I handed over to them. Nothing was ringing alarm bells that something was not right. They struggled to start, not unusual, so I asked how their day had been. In response I got a shrug and "Okay." I asked what thoughts they had had during the day about our session. In response, I was told they did not know they were coming. Pardon? What?! - I thought. I clarified my understanding that they were not aware of the session. At what point *did* they know? When they arrived home after school, they were told they were coming to counselling. They had time to change out of school uniform and then they were here. Wow. What a shock that must have been. How bewildered must they be feeling?

I explained the decision was 100% theirs as to whether they wanted to be here. I was aiming to give the client power, as it did not sound like they had much control or power over anything. If the client does not want to be here, then counselling is not going to work.

Their parent was waiting outside, so I asked if they wanted me to take them back to their parent. There was some hesitation on the client's part. I suggested it would be okay if they wanted to stay for a bit and talk or do something creative. To my surprise, they said they wanted to stay. They gave me an outline of what had been going on but were finished after about 20 minutes. I explained again that it is up to them, no one else but them, if they want to return. We then went back to the parent where I explained the same to them. I wanted to ask them what they thought they were playing at in springing a surprise like that on their child, but I did not. Perhaps the parent felt they were at their wit's end. Note to self, stop with the judgement!

I went back to the room and just sat there, in utter disbelief that a parent could do that to their child. I let my placement manager know. They said they make sure when they talk to the parent that their child is willing to come and engage in counselling. The client did not return.

When Clients Have Nothing To Say

At one point, it seemed client after client would start the session by declaring they had nothing they wanted to talk about. I found this a bit excruciating early on as felt the onus was on me to talk and ask question after question in an attempt to get the client talking and fill 50 minutes. I would sit there and wonder why they had turned up.

After getting some advice from supervision, I simply started by reflecting they had nothing to talk about and left a bit of silence (depending on age; silence and young people do not always work so tread carefully.) Sometimes a little silence would work, the client just needed to start slowly and gently. Sometimes the silence did not work. I would then move on to ask what had motivated them to come to the session. What had their day or week been like? This would usually then get the client talking. On the rare occasions where it did not, I would ask the client how they wanted to spend the time. This took a little getting used to until I felt comfortable in this situation. I just kept reminding myself that this is the client's time to talk, not mine.

Planning Goes Out The Window

Many a time I would have an outline plan in my head on how the next session might unfold and plan some things. This may include some research or thinking about a creative task that might be useful. However, a high percentage of the time the planning would fly out the window as the client either brought something new or started talking where I could not get a word in. This was a useful reminder to follow the client where they want to go.

Creativity

Before going on placement, I spent a small fortune on many things that I felt might come in useful. I bought things like emotion cards, shells, pens, crayons, paper, adult colouring books, post-it notes, mandala colouring books, mini wooden pegs (the outline was vaguely human), colourful mini figures that represent animals, adults, and children, most of which I never used. I downloaded from various websites lots of CBT sheets covering a range of things with which they could help.

Lugging all my stuff around once placement had started quickly became tiresome. A couple of people I met on placement had small trolleys with compartments (a bit like mobile hairdresser trolleys), a great idea and saves the arms aching from all the carrying. Just make sure you have a ramp if needed as it might be difficult getting it up and down stairs.

Of the things I had obtained, these are my top items, not too expensive and even free in one case.

Stones

I picked these up free from various beaches. I later added to these with different colours of shiny polished pebbles.

Used for – I used these to help plot and understand relationships and dynamics. Invite the client to pick a stone that represents them and place it down. Then they choose other stones that represent people in their lives and position them relative to themselves in terms of closeness. You can then talk about noticing a certain size, or colour of stone and whether the stone is close or distant to them to see what meaning the client has for these other people.

NAILING COUNSELLING TRAINING

This approach worked especially well with a young client who chose the largest stone and set it apart from the others. They then grouped the smaller stones at a noticeable distance from the large stone. When I asked what it symbolised, my client explained that the large stone represented their tall parent, while the smaller ones were other family members. This simple activity opened up a conversation about family dynamics, allowing them to express feeling small at times—something that might not have surfaced through conversation alone.

Picture Cards
I bought some emotion cards and decided to make my own image cards after hearing a peer mention how they used a laminator to make their picture cards. I bought a cheap laminator and printed out some photos I had taken. It turned out to be invaluable, giving me the freedom to create custom cards rather than purchasing pre-made ones. There is also something incredibly soothing about sliding a picture into the plastic sleeve and watching it emerge warm and perfectly sealed on the other side.

Used for – Helping clients connect with their interpretation of the picture and express thoughts and feelings. Ask which pictures stand out for them, and then you can explore why this is and what it means. I also found it useful to simply get a sense of what they might like and dislike.

Fidget Toys
I bought a small box of assorted fidget toys of varying sizes, textures, colours, shapes, and some that made a noise. I included a soft stress ball and a Splatman, which I love. This proved good for letting out frustration and anger and was fun!

I invited one of my clients who always played with fidget toys in our sessions to take something at our last session and they chose my beloved Splatman. I was sorry to see it go, but happy it was going to be well used instead of stuck in my bag all week.

Used for – I had a couple of clients with autism and they both found it useful to just play with the fidget toys while speaking. Splatman was thrown against the wall many times with shrieks of joy from the young person every time it stuck to the wall and helped them express feelings of frustration.

I ended one session with a client by playing catch with the stress ball in the corridor. No one else was in the building and they had been throwing the ball against the room walls by themselves, so I asked if I could join in and then we just moved into the corridor. We had a fun time, lots of laughing and running around when I kept missing the ball.

I never thought I would be able to do something like that with a client. If it is appropriate to your client and situation, invite them to try an activity. Counselling does not have to be confined to sitting and talking.

Drawing
One client was happy to draw using just paper and felt tip pens or crayons.

Used for – Helping the client to express themselves when words are too difficult. Seeing something visual is often more helpful than verbally describing something. When we covered the more creative side of the course, our tutor said that we should always ask the client what they want to do with whatever it is they have produced, as it is their work.

NAILING COUNSELLING TRAINING

Masks
A great way to express the various masks we wear in life or hide behind.

Used for – When clients say they do not know who they are, or that they wear their game face and do not show their true selves to specific people or circumstances. I invite the client to draw or write, however they want to express how they feel, on the mask. The outside is for the face they show the world. The inside of the mask is what they keep hidden. Some really powerful things came out of this activity.

Nesting Dolls
Similar to above, just a different way to explore different parts of self. I opted for plain dolls rather than the traditional colourful ones as I wanted to keep it simple and not have the colourful decoration cause a distraction.

Used for – Helping clients to understand parts of self and the different layers we have, from the outside to the hidden inner inside and a few layers in between. I found this a good visual to work from. If the client wants to write or draw rather than talk, I additionally have outlines of the nesting dolls with their assorted sizes on paper.

Conversation starter cubes
Soft cubes, like dice that you roll, with a different question written on each side.

Used for – These are a good icebreaker if the client is finding it difficult to start talking about what brings them to counselling.

I had a client who did not know how to start. They were nervous, embarrassed, and laughing and just could not get any words out. I explained what the cubes were and invited the client to pick one to roll. It was a simple enough question about favourite food. This immediately took the pressure off of why the client had come, and I could see the client looked grateful to focus on something else. I joined in answering as well to help build a rapport, and after a few more questions and a little laughter, the client was much more relaxed and was able to hesitatingly speak about why they wanted to talk to someone.

I took this to supervision, as being a newbie, I was terrified of pretty much anything I did at this point, so was not sure if my participation fell under self-disclosure, and if that was the right thing to do. My supervisor simply said that it sounded like it was needed. The client needed to know something about me, even if it was my favourite food, to see my willingness to join in, so that they could then open up to me.

Emotion wheels
I used Google a lot for ideas of things to try. I took inspiration from an idea I saw which was to create my own 'Anger wheel.' It simply has the word anger in large letters and below this in a wheel formation are emotions, thoughts and feelings that might be behind the anger, e.g. hurt, grief, loneliness, and shame. When someone is angry, they do not necessarily know how to break that down into understandable chunks, so the Anger Wheel came in useful a few times.

You can then create others, such as one for anxiety. That is another hard one for people to describe so having suggestions of what might be behind the anxiety makes it easier for the client to start unpacking their issues.

A feelings wheel is another useful example. You could also see if your client wants to produce their design as they identify the thoughts, feelings, and emotions behind their issues.

Distractions

Prepare for some distractions! Quite early on I was still extremely nervous, the window was open a little as it was summer, and the room was hot. An annoying fly decided to fly in and buzz around my client and me. I am sitting there wondering whether to mention it or ignore it. I was agonising over what to do about a fly! My client started swatting it, so I joined in, and we had a laugh and continued with the session. Neither of us noticed when it stopped being a nuisance.

Another time, just as a client was getting to something important and deep, we heard the cheery tones of an ice cream van. Such timing! It did break the moment a little, all I could do was apologise.

The room I was using faced the car park and at certain times, always mid-session, a van would reverse into its dedicated space so we would always hear the beep beep beep. Lesson learned, wherever you do your counselling, check for potential distractions, and consider how you might mitigate or manage them.

My Tinder Alert System

Other distractions for me came in the form of my thoughts when I was with a client. Random thoughts might enter my head or be triggered by something the client has said which meant that I was not fully listening to my client.

There may also be times when you are thinking about a client you have just seen or the client you will see after the current one. Anything can and probably will come into your mind when you do not want it to.

I am not sure how this happened, but one day I was aware that I took my thought, and visualised swiping it left, out of my mind forever. If I swiped my thought right, it meant I was parking it for later to reflect on. That meant my mind could be kept free to focus on my clients. The Tinder Alert System continues to serve me well today!

Swearing Clients

Your clients might swear! I think that a couple of my clients swore deliberately to see if I would react. For other clients, it seemed a natural way for them to speak. Personally, I am not offended by swearing. If this is an issue for you, you may want to think about how you might react in the moment.

Did Not Attend (DNA)

These are where the client does not attend and does not let you know. I had lots of these. Depending on whether the client is a child or adult, and what you might have agreed at contracting, you are likely to need to contact them. You want to know that primarily they are okay. If they are late, is it still feasible for the session to go ahead (they may live 5 minutes away) but still end at the original time? Otherwise, it is to re-arrange the session or end the counselling sessions if that is what the client wants.

My placement had a strict policy for DNAs that I found challenging to enforce. If clients missed an appointment without giving 24 hours' notice, their sessions would be terminated. I thought this was harsh. Life is hectic—people forget, get stuck in traffic, or apologise sincerely and ask to reschedule. I would refer them to the signed contract and remind them of the rules, but I was always unsure if my wording was coming across as a reprimand. I needed them to understand the consequences without feeling scolded. I also thought about the people on the waiting list who were further delayed because of repeated no-shows. Perhaps the client was struggling to attend or finding therapy difficult. I frequently discussed my difficulties in managing the rules of DNA according to the client's circumstances with my placement manager and supervisor, trying to understand why this was so hard for me to implement.

Where Are Your Clients?

If you are not doing face-to-face counselling, it will be useful to ask your clients where they are when doing telephone and video work. Are they comfortable, in a safe and confidential space, and not be overheard? This gives you an idea of their wider environment if there are occasions where you need to call the next of kin or emergency services, so ensure you know the address they are at.

Supervision

Supervision/Client Ratio
You will most likely need to follow a specific supervision/client ratio for supervision. For my placement, I

joined the BACP as a student member. This meant I needed to have 1.5 hours minimum supervision per month, ideally a supervision session every 2 weeks. The person doing the supervision has to be a qualified supervisor. The ratio I had to follow was 1 hour of supervision for every eight client hours.

For group supervision, try to limit to no more than four peers for an hour's supervision. That way you can claim half the time. If there are five peers then you divide the total time by five, and so on.

It is a lot to get your head around, especially when you start taking on more placement clients. If any client hours exceed the supervision rules, chances are you will lose those hours and cannot claim them as part of the 100-hour placement.

Get A Great Supervisor
I cannot emphasise this enough – get yourself a really good supervisor. My private one came courtesy of a peer recommendation. I immediately liked this supervisor, and it is rare for me to make an instant decision about someone.

I had my first supervision session before seeing my first client, so that I could talk about the intake, what it might mean and where the conversation might go, how prepared I felt, and that kind of thing. That was helpful, and I would recommend doing that if you can.

I stayed with this supervisor throughout my placement, feeling well supported and listened to. I felt that I could be completely honest about whether I liked or disliked a client, and whether I made mistakes, all with no judgement. My supervisor challenged me, and I felt like I could tell them anything.

NAILING COUNSELLING TRAINING

It was pointed out to me when I first encountered transference and countertransference with a client and the impact this may have had. Throughout my placement I experienced these a lot. With one client, they expressed an interest in science and technology which is my background. I explored this with them as I was interested in their ideas and how they resonated with me, and my supervisor pointed out that I had not explored what else the client might enjoy. Gah! Another time, I was left with feelings of sheer exasperation with an adult client talking about being bullied. I could see the victim role they were in and I just wanted to shake them and say they can turn this around instead of wallowing. But it was only when my supervisor pressed me for *why* I felt this way, that I realised I was reacting based on my own experiences. I was thinking about how much of my adult life I had been in similar situations and was angry and frustrated at myself. Once I was aware of this and in session with the client, I was able to swipe anything that came up for me to the right to deal with later and focus on the client. Yay for the Tinder Alert System!

Having a great supervisor during training was priceless to my learning and increasing levels of confidence.

Peer Supervision
As long as an experienced supervisor is facilitating this, I found the experience useful. Learning about the clients that my peers had and how they were supporting their clients was a good aid to my learning. Also having the opportunity to provide feedback was good. Just be aware of group size for how much supervision time you can claim.

There was one instance that has made me wary of peer supervision. A couple of people knew me, so maybe they were frank in what they said because of this. They ignored the difficulties I said I was having with a certain client and dismissed my feelings about not wanting to continue working with them, telling me "I *should*" as everyone else has let this person down and they keep coming back to me for a reason. There were lots of "I should" and "I need to" and this was provoking real anger within me, especially as we had covered the negative thinking patterns of "I should" statements on the course! I felt like I was being emotionally blackmailed, that the client's wellbeing was down to me, and me alone. I was being ignored. It was only a third person, whom I did not know, who said they could hear me, and validated my experience and offered to explore my feelings.

So, beware of peer supervision, especially during training as inexperienced peers may project onto you. Hopefully, any peer session will be moderated by a qualified supervisor who can interject if needed.

My Issues Coming Up…. Again!

When I had young people talking about fitting in, body image and peer pressure, that triggered my uncomfortable feelings and fear. They are saying this to someone sitting opposite them who is overweight, wearing clothes that are years old, with grey frizzy hair tied back and wearing no makeup. Do my clients even *see me*, I often wondered during my placement. My thoughts would be, how can I support this issue when I do not fit a social construct of perfection myself?

I grew up in a generation of children that had unlocked front doors. I was always playing outside at every opportunity with neighbourhood kids, climbing trees, spraining ankles, running, cycling, very physically active. There was no internet, four channels on TV and imagination was used to play games. Therefore, trying to relate to today's young people's issues around appearance, peer judgement and social media pressures was a new experience which I found difficult to relate to. Most of the time I just wanted to scream out that they are wasting precious time and energy on this unimportant stuff that could be better focussed elsewhere, why can't they see that?! Love yourself and accept yourself for who you are, not what someone else says you should be. Even though I found these interactions difficult, it is about sitting with the client and listening to how it affects them and helping them find ways forward, which differed from client to client.

Being Used By A Client

I was seeing a young person, who refused to go to school most days. During one session we talked about what days the client had gone to school that week. I suddenly twigged that the client did not seem to attend school the day of and after counselling. When I queried this, they responded with a smile that their mental health deteriorates after counselling. I accept counselling can bring up things in the coming days or weeks, but given our interactions, and the times they had nothing to say, I was highly suspicious that I was being used as a reason to justify not attending school for one or two days per week.

We were near the end of sessions and I felt like a fool, so I did not explore this with the client. I am not sure I wanted my suspicions confirmed. This was another one to work through in supervision.

Asking For Advice

I had some clients that would directly ask me for advice. I found it slightly awkward at first to seamlessly reflect this in a way that did not seem jarring to our interaction. I would usually get a feel for how best to respond. Sometimes I would ask my client what advice they wanted to hear. That often prompted the client to say what they thought was best, so I would then explore that with the client. Other times I would ask the client what choices they felt they had, helping them explore those. If it felt applicable I would offer a reminder that counselling is not about me giving them advice.

Bring It Into The Room

During the Level 4 training, my tutor would frequently say "Bring it into the room". This was about anything different between our clients and ourselves. I never really understood this. What did that even mean? Was I supposed to say, "I notice the difference in our size, height, hair colour, skin colour"?!

When I first encountered a client with ADHD, I did not "bring it into the room." I paid no heed to their diagnosis, put it to one side and did not appreciate how this affected the client. My good intentions were to support the client as best as I could, but how could I when I would feel annoyed they were late again and not consider how ADHD affected them daily, or in a counselling session that they might find stressful? It was only when I was a little further into my placement hours when I had a client with autism that it clicked. We spent much of the first session discussing how autism affected them, how they could be comfortable in the room with me, and what I could do to help with this. For instance, my client could not maintain eye contact for long and would stare at the wall, so I offered to frequently look away. In everything that was said by my client and myself, I held autism at the forefront of my mind. For the last couple of sessions with my ADHD client, I was able to now bring it into the room, but I wished I could have had a complete do-over with this client, or better still, refer them to a counsellor experienced with working with ADHD.

Recognising A Client's Parent

Once, when seeing a client out, I realised their parent (whom I had not met at the first session) looked vaguely familiar as I watched my client walk across the car park to be collected. He looked like someone who worked at the same company as me (in my day job). I panicked internally, had he seen me? How should I handle this? As soon as I got to work the next morning, I looked him up on the company intranet. The picture was old and a bit grainy, so I had to zoom in quite a bit. As I was staring intently at this zoomed-in picture, trying to decide if it was him, I was aware someone had come into the lab where I was working and was standing behind me going through the toolbox. I turned around... and yes... it was him! Cue lots of internal groaning and wishing the ground would swallow me up. Had he seen me staring intently at his picture?!

I took this to supervision as I was wondering about a conflict of interest. Assuming it was him, did he recognise me? I am sure he will be wondering what on earth I am doing counselling his child. No one at work knows I am studying counselling, do I need to tell him? My supervisor's advice is to wait and see if he says anything. We ponder if there is there a conflict of interest as we work at the same company, but not together, which has nothing to do with his child or what I do in my own time.

The building I worked in had some narrow corridors and it seemed every time I left the lab to go somewhere we passed each other. I search his face to see if he is looking at me oddly, I smile and try to appear open if he wants to say something. In hindsight, probably not the best move given I was possibly caught staring at his picture!!

During another session with my client, they mentioned what their father does for a living... oh good news, it was not him after all. So now I just live with the fact that a work colleague might have seen me staring intently at his zoomed-in picture and I suddenly started smiling at him every time we pass each other!

As embarrassing and amusing as this was for me, it proved a good point. If your placement is near your home, work, or in the area where you may bump into someone you know in the context of actively doing your placement, how might you handle the situation?

Dealing With Parents/Primary Caregivers

At my placement, I was encouraged to give the young person agency and autonomy. Therefore, when meeting them for the first time I would explain there is a contract and other forms to go through and if they are comfortable doing this then their parent can leave and come back in 50 minutes. All my young people and parents were okay with this so usually I would spend about a minute or two with the parent before seeing them off.

It did not hit me until near the end of my placement how much trust a parent is putting in me to be with their child. I needed to speak to a parent, with the young person's permission and they were also present. The way the parent accepted what I was saying, asking questions, and seeking reassurance, I realised their default setting was they assumed I was capable and trustworthy to be with their child. Recognising that in most cases I spend limited time with the parent at the door, focusing mostly on their child before they leave, I felt quite humble at that point.

Dealing With Other Agencies

This subject is a major bone of contention for me. At the start of embarking on counselling training, I thought it would be useful to get a counselling job within the NHS. As I have since learned, that is not going to happen unless I pay to do further courses in CBT or undertake training in Improving Access to Psychological Therapies (IAPT), now known as NHS Talking Therapies, for anxiety and depression. I do not know if the name change to talking therapies now means non-CBT counselling is offered, but certainly, at one point it seemed that regardless of issues, the only therapy offered was CBT.

As I have not completed the training the NHS require, I am not good enough to work with clients who have been referred within the NHS for counselling. However, as an unpaid trainee at a charity, I am good enough to work with these people. Madness! These clients would be referred to the charity if the NHS services decided they could not support them. I have also worked with clients who came to me after being referred from the NHS to a third-party partnership who also declared they were unable to work with the client. One particular client was offered CBT, but it was decided that they needed to "talk through their issues" before CBT started. I was able to support this person and then had to reluctantly refer them back so they could get CBT. It was clear to me that they would benefit from further talking.

So that is the sore point. I am not good enough to work with the NHS in a paid position, but I am good enough as an unpaid trainee.

All the while I was supported by both my placement manager and supervisor and could decline to work with any clients I felt I was out of my depth with, at any point. These clients were also made aware of my experience so could choose whether to continue seeing me.

A point to note, if you do belong to a membership organisation post-qualifying that is on the PSA-accredited register, this means you have been evaluated to meet certain standards. This in turn means you are deemed good enough to be able to work with clients who go via the NHS!

Client Gifts

At the last session with one client, I was presented with a beautiful, homemade gift. I was floored to have received this and felt refusal would have been insulting. After expressing many thanks, I placed the gift out of the way, and we had our final session.

I took that to supervision, and we explored how I felt receiving a gift, what was the placement policy, whether I would do anything differently if another client brought me a gift, and what may have motivated my client to do that for me.

Given the incident that had occurred with the non-qualified 'supervisor' during my class supervision session on Level 4, my private supervisor suggested I take a picture and stick it up somewhere I will frequently see it. It would serve as a reminder of how wrong that person was, that what I had done for my client had led them to do that for me. Therefore, I dutifully took a picture, laminated it, and placed it where I see it frequently. When I take time to study the picture I always smile when I think of the client and sometimes have to pinch myself that they did that for me.

In general, I would not refuse a client's gift as that would seem like a rejection. If the gift is chocolates or flowers, you could always say you will share the chocolates with the other staff, and put the flowers on reception, something like that if you are not allowed, or do not feel comfortable taking the gift home. It could be that your placement has a policy for not accepting gifts that could be mentioned in the contract, that way it takes the personal out of the situation.

Theory Coming Into Play

The theory learned during Level 3 was starting to click into place. I identified Carl Roger's conditions of worth and worked with this quite a bit with a few clients. Attachment styles were also really useful, whether I simply noted these to aid me, or explored this with the client.

I did some high-level CBT at times, so some psychoeducation around thoughts > feelings > behaviour and doing a little work with this.

Existentialism also came up, and in some of this content, my client and I worked creatively to help make sense of their place in the world. It was certainly good to see that I had paid attention in class.

As much as the theory was important and gave me things I could draw on, I was more focused on building the relationship between my client and myself first. I now understand Carl Jung's quote:

Know all the theories, master all the techniques, but as you touch a human soul just be another human soul.

I enjoyed the freedom of delving into different models and approaches to mix and match strategies of what I felt would be useful for my clients, rather than having to stick to one approach. That shows that being an integrative counsellor is what I want to be.

Anger Issues

One of my clients, an adult male, presented with depression at intake. At our first session, however, it was obvious that anger was bubbling just below the surface. This was the only client I worked with where I eyeballed the door and attempted to calculate whether I could beat my client to the door. Whilst my chair was nearer the door, he had youth and fitness on his side. I did not feel personally threatened, my spidey senses were not red-flagging me, but I wanted reassurance that I could swiftly exit the room if anger appeared. I was also trying to think if anyone else was in the building.

There were no safety issues in that session. I spoke to my placement manager and said I did not feel comfortable seeing this client, and the client did not return, which I felt relieved about.

Going forward, I would always make sure to find out if anyone else was working in the building, and which rooms they were in, and I made sure to re-read the lone worker policy. I found it easy to just get caught up in arriving on time, preparing the room, and reading through notes, that I would not have time to consider who else might be around if I needed assistance.

Counting Down The One Hundred Placement Hours

When I first started at my placement, I met other trainee counsellors who were almost at the end of their required one hundred hours. Now I had finally started at my placement that I could not envisage a year ago, I had moved onto struggling to envisage reaching the 100th client hour. One evening, a trainee had a client who DNA and was feeling frustrated. This was expressed as "That's just cost me an hour." I remember feeling a "whoa!" moment. Is that all they saw their clients as, just hours to tick off? I hoped I would never see my clients like that.

Well, fast-forward to when I reached about 95 hours. It is hard when you are so close to the end not to get carried away and think "This time next week I will have completed all my hours." I had a couple of DNAs at the end, and yes, I admit to the occasional feeling of "You've just cost me an hour!!"

Some trainees like to mark off each hour as a countdown to finishing. I chose to continue adding a marble to a large jar for each client, not each client hour, which I had started when I first began my bereavement volunteer role. I have seen some innovative ideas that other people shared online, such as a special 100-piece jigsaw puzzle that counts off numbers 1 – 100. There is also simply putting aside £1 for each hour completed and at the end the person treats themselves to something nice. Another nice idea is to write down one reflective thought per client hour and then read it back after one hundred hours have been reached. There are so many ways you can mark off this achievement and get something good out of the end result.

Endings

At my placement interview, I was told that although we are taught about the importance of endings during training, we do not always get them. This turned out to be a rather accurate comment for me. I had some clients who did not even turn up, so no beginning either, and some clients who did not come back after the first, second, or third session. I do not know why, so there is no closure there. You can drive yourself crazy by forensically going over every word that was said that might have annoyed the client or wondering if they did not like you. However, I have accepted that sometimes it is just not meant to be. Maybe it is something about me. Maybe the client realises they are not ready or that counselling is not for them. I do not take it personally and move on to the next client. Supervision is great for working through that.

Most of my clients stayed the course so we would start to plan the ending a few sessions beforehand. For example, getting it on the client's weekly radar that we are at session 3 of 12, 4 of 12, etc, and emphasising the number of sessions left, so they are not surprised. Most of my younger clients had no idea and just shrugged when asked how they wanted it to end.

Some of my clients were not happy the end was coming. We had built a good therapeutic relationship, it had become routine, so gently exploring what the client might do with their time, who might they go to if they want to talk to someone, and what strategies have they learned to help them was useful to go over.

I had mixed feelings, some I was okay with not seeing again, and some I knew I would miss. Some I still think of now and again. Another one to talk through with your supervisor.

Client Issues I Worked With

These are the types of issues I was confronted with on placement. Some issues were limited to one thing with a client, other clients presented with multiple issues. In those instances, the client and I would explore the relationship between the issues, and possible cause and effect, to help the client figure out where they might want to start. To better educate myself on some of the issues, I spent lots of time on Google, finding specialist charity websites, seeking guidance from my supervisor and placement manager for information on the subject matter, how I might support someone and whether I was the right person for the client.

- Attention Deficit Hyperactivity Disorder (ADHD)
- Stress
- Anxiety
- Self-Harming
- School Avoidant
- Anger
- Peer Judgement
- Workplace Bullying
- Rape
- Sexual Assault
- Coercive Control
- Sleep Anxiety
- Grooming
- Social Media Pressure
- Low Self Esteem
- School Bullying
- Appearance
- Blackmail
- Bereavement
- Oppositional Defiant Disorder (ODD)
- Relationship Issues
- Loss of Identity
- Suicide Ideation
- Depression

I think my most challenging experience was trying to form a therapeutic relationship with a client who had ODD and be able to show them the core counselling skills. I had not heard of this condition and had to google what it was about. The old me would have called them a difficult person, and at times I was on the verge of declaring I could not continue to work with them. I took them to supervision a lot, and instead of saying I had a "difficult client," I found myself saying "The client *I* was having difficulty with." Quite a growth point for me.

Placement Admin

I aimed to complete my course paperwork for the counselling and supervision hours logs every week. There were times I did not do this, and it can get messy quite quickly. For instance, if I had not yet updated my diary to show a client was a DNA then I would count them, and when cross-referencing the forms my numbers would not add up. The paperwork can be a nightmare, my advice is to keep on top of it.

My Self-Care

I needed an outlet for the things I heard from my clients, some of which stuck with me for a long time. My usual go-to activities were not enough. There were times when I needed my mind to be filled by something else entirely. My chosen activity was to learn songs in British Sign Language (BSL). I had taken a BSL course so already knew some sign language and enjoyed learning songs as the repetitive chorus was good to help me learn new signs. This is something I do alone and requires 100% concentration so that I can lose myself in the lyrics and the signs. After a BSL song session, I felt calmer and more able to rationalise what client issues were sticking in my mind so I could then process my thoughts and either swipe right to park for supervision or swipe left to discard them.

I knew a couple of BSL songs at the start of Level 3. Now, after qualifying as a counsellor, I know about ten songs.

This was a difficult year to get through, dealing with these issues and never knowing if I was doing more harm than good. Some clients I laughed along with; others broke my heart. I spent many sleepless nights thinking about them, and many days carrying them in my head. But it was worth it, and I am glad I have had this experience.

NOTES

NOTES

~ *Chapter 8* ~
Post-Qualifying Changes

Where Am I Now?

I am a qualified integrative counsellor working in private practice in the UK, specialising in short and long-term counselling for adults aged 18+.

Sadly, the majority of issues my clients presented me with I have lived experience of also. I managed to get through those times. I know it will not be the same experience for everyone, but I have an insight into what it feels like to go through most things my placement clients have also experienced.

I ended my last reflective journal from the course on self-awareness with this quote. I love it and think it is spot on, so this is what I aim for when I am with a client:

"It is not about me treating or curing or trying to change someone, it is about how I provide a relationship which this person may use for his personal growth" - Carl Rogers

If you are looking for a counsellor and I sound like someone you may be able to work with, then please visit my website for how to get in touch. I offer reduced rates for student counsellors as I know the cost of training is expensive.

www.centredmindscounselling.co.uk

Looking Back

I look back at my life now and have sometimes been quite hard on myself for not doing this sooner. Why did I allow myself to get stuck in a rut and spend so many years that was quite frankly, unhappy? However, I will be kind and forgiving to myself. I simply was not ready to embark on this experience earlier. Now feels like the right time. I have a wealth of life experience to go with my qualifications, and through this experience, I have grown as a person.

I am now proactive about a future I want, rather than just reacting to people and circumstances and feeling like I am just bumbling through life with no hope or purpose.

It is interesting to me that I can still have those immediate, knee-jerk, negative reactions to things. Was I expecting that I would somehow achieve a high and permanent level of calm and understanding after qualifying? I still think and feel in unhelpful ways. I am not always calm. I still feel sad and low at times. I know these feelings will pass. Feeling sad or depressed does not make me a sad or depressed person, it is a temporary state. What I can do now, is think about why these moods and feelings occur.

How Have I Changed?

Counselling training has changed me from a person who did not have much confidence and liked sticking to what I knew felt safe, rather than experiencing new things, to someone who is now full of confidence. I passed a counselling course that was difficult at times. I completed and loved my face-to-face placement. I set up my own business and authored this book!

It has taken a few years to get here, but I have now arrived at a place in my life where I am happy and thriving.

The opportunity I had during the counselling training, to be honest with myself, connect my thoughts and feelings and listen and trust in myself, is priceless. This personal development is very much ongoing.

I am less judgemental and assumptive and more reflective in my thinking. I am more self-aware and no longer strive to be a people-fixer. I am accepting of good enough in place of perfection.

I am still scatty at times, have retained my dark sense of humour (which at times feels like it keeps me sane) and still like silly jokes. Have you read Freud's Jokes and Their Relation to the Unconscious? I wonder what Freud would have made of these:

How many counsellors does it take to change a lightbulb?

One, but only if the lightbulb really wants to change!

And.

Ego and Superego walk into a pub. The bartender says, "I need to see id."

Relationships

Past, current, and future relationships were reflected upon, especially from Level 3 onwards as that is where I felt myself growing as a person. This did mean that I looked at other aspects of my life through a different lens, coming to the realisation that some relationships were not in my best interests, and I held my hands up to the part I played in those.

Myself

My relationship with myself has transformed significantly. While maladaptive thoughts still surface from time to time, I have developed the ability to recognise them and reflect on why they emerge.

Going into my 100-hour placement, my greatest fear was being judged and rejected by the teenagers I would be working with. In the past, I often felt overlooked in my career, sometimes to the point of wondering if I had become invisible—and I attributed all of this to my weight. Now, I acknowledge that there may have been some truth to that, and there likely will be in the future. However, I have realised that I spent years projecting my own negative, judgmental thoughts onto others, rarely giving them a chance to prove me right or wrong.

Surprisingly to me, not one of the clients in my placement seemed to reject me, and I was able to form strong therapeutic relationships with most of them. The gradual process of unpacking my inner psyche has been eye-opening. I now imagine myself in a duel with these negative thoughts, skilfully parrying and slicing through the false meanings and assumptions I have carried for so long, before plunging the sword into the final whispers of self-doubt and inadequacy and feeling them fade away. The feeling of vanquishing those thoughts is incredibly liberating.

Family
I am sure I listen and respond a bit differently now. However, I am a daughter and a sister, and quite happy with the status quo with my family.

Existing Friendships
I would say as a direct result of the counselling course that I lost three friends. I mulled over past relationships, being able to identify the roles that were being played out with me and the other person. In most cases I can see that actually, the relationship was not necessarily a healthy one, as I tended to play a secondary role to the other person. A harsh, but useful insight and awareness to have.

Other existing friendships have continued to strengthen and deepen. When thinking about these, I have a sense of ease and acceptance about them. I accept them and they accept me. Now, I can accept that I am a likeable person who people want to be around. They are not using me for their purposes to get something out of me, they are genuine. I get value from having these people in my life.

There have been occasions where issues crop up for friends. Early on after qualifying, as I listened, I wondered if I was being a friend or a counsellor. I would not do counselling with family or friends and found my mind would feel split between the two in how to respond. If things come up now, I am happy to listen and support them as a friend, but they know it is not a counselling session. I no longer experience the conflict in my mind, being a counsellor is not a side part of me that I can switch on or off, it is ingrained in me.

NAILING COUNSELLING TRAINING

New Friends
I have often wondered what making new relationships with people might look like now I have changed. If I say I am a counsellor, will that put people off or draw people in because they want some free counselling, using that as a guise to be friends?

I am fortunate to have grown my friend base with some people from my counselling course. It can be very lonely being a counsellor. You cannot go home at the end of the day and chat about what happened with family, due to client confidentiality. Upsetting things can sit with you and impact your day, I have even cancelled plans at short notice a couple of times as I was just not in the mood. The only other person you can talk to in-depth is your supervisor, so having other like-minded friends that you can go to, who simply understand, is just fantastic.

With the issue I encountered having my ability to be a counsellor questioned, some people witnessed it and offered no support, and some people took a deliberate step back to distance themselves. What I have learned is that the people who step forward in your time of need, at a possible cost to themselves, who offer compassion and non-judgement, are keepers. So, I will certainly do my best to nurture those relationships as these are the friends I want in my life.

Significant Other
I did not go into my counselling training with a significant other, so no insight to provide there. However, I do hear that often going through a counselling course can lead to trainees questioning the future of their relationships. Those relationships already in a fragile state may end or get stronger, so prepare for close personal relationships to change.

Sitting With A Client

I have been asked what it is like to be in session with a client now I am qualified. This pretty much sums it up:

I am *present* in every session, mentally and emotionally. I am alert for any safeguarding issues. I am the sole keeper of secrets. I am *listening* for fifty minutes with intense focus. My client may find it upsetting. They may cry. I have to *manage the emotions*. I may want to cry also but cannot. I have to *hold my emotions in silence*. I do not move much aside from subtle movements to manage muscle stiffness. I do not allow myself to become distracted. My Tinder Alert System makes sure of that. I am *not solving their pain,* I am present by their side, *holding their pain* without flinching. I cannot get in too deep as I must remain objective to be of service. For fifty minutes I am working out a *mental puzzle*. I am reflecting, empathising, and synthesising internally. I am trying to make sense of everything that has been said, and what the body language might be telling me. I am *tracking themes* and pulling together the narrative from seemingly unrelated things that were said. I remember the dynamics at play in their life and how this impacts them. I am *deciding* on a therapeutic direction which may change during the fifty minutes. I am keeping a check on *time* so that I can bring them to a state where they can safely leave the session. After our time is up I move to loosen muscles. I *distil fifty minutes'* worth of information and consider what notes I need to make. I have a drink, maybe a snack if there is time. I check messages and act on any I need to. I pray that there is no crisis to attend to that involves me or impacts the next client. I go over my responses, *questioning* whether I said the right thing. I find a way to put that client *out of my mind*. I prepare for my next client. *I do it all again* for the next client. And the next. I do this day in, and day out ***because I want to***.

If I were to sum up the experience of going through counselling training in a sentence, it would be something like, "Coming out the end of counselling training meant I was finally able to reclaim myself."

~ *Chapter 9* ~
Useful Training Resources

The following resources continue to help me understand more about counselling, people, and resilience.

Digital

Consider listening to Podcasts, YouTube, Spotify, etc.

Books

Man's Search for Meaning – Viktor E. Frankl

The Choice – Edith Eger

Wave – Sonali Deraniyagala

The Whole-Brain Childaa – Dr Daniel J. Siegel and Dr Tina Payne Bryson

Maybe you should talk to someone – Lori Gottlieb

On Becoming a Person, A Therapist's View of Psychotherapy – Carl Rogers

The Gift of Therapy – Irvin D. Yalom

Love's Executioner – Irvin D. Yalom

The Skilled Helper – Gerard Egan

The Grieving Brain – Mary-Frances O'Connor, PhD

Who Moved My Cheese - Dr Spencer Johnson

Integrative Counselling Skills in Action – Sue Cully & Tim Bond

Unshame – Carolyn Spring

The Body Keeps the Score – Bessel Van Der Kolk

My Favourite Books
The Body Keeps the Score

I find this an invaluable resource because it explores the profound impact of trauma on both the mind and body. It provides insights into how trauma manifests physically and emotionally, emphasising the importance of understanding these connections in counselling practice. Be mindful that there is some criticism of this book around anecdotal evidence, simplification of complex issues and controversial approaches, so this is a good book to evaluate critically and research.

My takeaway is that it gives me an opening to holistically address the complexities of trauma for the mind and body. I particularly like explanations and examples of how the brain's amygdala and limbic systems affect how we respond to trauma, fear and processing emotions:

The Amygdala is the brain's "smoke detector," constantly scanning for threats. When it senses danger, it triggers the body's fight-or-flight response, releasing stress hormones like adrenaline and cortisol. This happens very quickly and often before the rational brain (the prefrontal cortex) has time to evaluate the situation.

The limbic system, which includes the amygdala, is responsible for regulating emotions, memory, and arousal. When trauma occurs, the amygdala can become overactive, leading to heightened states of fear and anxiety, even when there is no actual danger. This can explain why trauma survivors often feel stuck in a state of hypervigilance or emotional dysregulation.

The Grieving Brain

I came across this book during my bereavement counsellor volunteer role. I love how it combines neuroscience and psychology to explore how grief impacts the brain and body. The book offers insights into the grieving process, highlighting its complexity and the individual variations in how people experience loss.

My takeaway is being able to understand the neuroscience elements of grief, as the author uses easy-to-understand language.

Man's Search for Meaning

I came across this book many years ago when I wanted to learn more about World War 2, way before counselling was on my radar. It delves into the profound impact of finding purpose and meaning in life, even amidst suffering and adversity. The author was a psychiatrist and researching logotherapy (the search for meaning is the primary human motivation) as a therapeutic approach before he was sent to a concentration camp.

My takeaway is understanding the importance of personal meaning and hope, which can be instrumental in helping clients navigate their struggles.

The Choice

I came across this book as part of my research into World War 2, offering insights into the human capacity for resilience and healing after trauma, following Edith's experience of being in a concentration camp. The author became a psychologist, helping others to heal their trauma.

My takeaway is understanding the power of choice in helping clients overcome suffering and find meaning to reclaim their lives and agency in the face of adversity.

Wave

I came across this book while searching for stories on grief and loss. This is a very intimate and raw account of the author's experience of losing her family in the 2004 tsunami, describing the overwhelming nature of loss and the struggle to find meaning in the aftermath.

My takeaway is another example of the resilience of the human spirit, after the experiences of trauma and grief.

Author's Note

Thank you so much for making it to the end of this book. I truly appreciate the time and energy you have invested in reading my work, and I hope you found it insightful and useful on your journey.

It has been a deeply personal process for me, and knowing it's reached you means a lot. If even a small part of this book resonated with you, then it has served its purpose.

I wish you all the best in whatever steps you take next. Thank you again for being here.

~ *References* ~

NAILING COUNSELLING TRAINING

Finding A Course Provider

www.gov.uk/government/organisations/ofqual/about

www.gov.uk/find-a-regulated-qualification

www.professionalstandards.org.uk

Which Route To Take

https://nationalcareers.service.gov.uk

www.ucas.com/careers-advice/how-to-become/counsellor

www.open.ac.uk/courses/careers/counselling

www.gov.uk/advanced-learner-loan

Measurement Counselling Tools

www.bacp.co.uk/media/18410/bacp-pre-post-outcomes-tool-guidance-v4-aug23.pdf

Information On Counselling Skills

www.simplypsychology.org/client-centred-therapy.html

Ethical Framework

www.bacp.co.uk/events-and-resources/ethics-and-standards

www.ncps.com/about-us/code-of-ethics

Personal Awareness Frameworks

www.therapyhub.eu/johari-window-a-simple-tool-for-self-awareness

www.simplypsychology.org/maslow.html

Counselling Models – Humanistic

www.youtube.com/watch?v=m30jsZx_Ngs

www.simplypsychology.org/client-centred-therapy.html

www.simplypsychology.org/conditions-of-worth.html

www.positivepsychology.com/rogers-actualizing-tendency
(*I love this potato story, scroll down to 'What is Actualising Tendency.'*)

www.yalom.com/biography

www.psychosynthesistrust.org.uk/about-the-psychosynthesis-trust/about-psychosynthesis

www.gestaltcentre.org.uk/what-is-gestalt

www.positivepsychology.com/gestalt-therapy

www.simplypsychology.org/transactional-analysis-eric-berne.html

Counselling Models – Non-Humanistic

www.beckinstitute.org/about/dr-aaron-t-beck

www.albertellis.org/rebt-cbt-therapy

www.freud.org.uk

www.annafreud.org

www.simplypsychology.org/psychosexual.html

www.simplypsychology.org/psyche.html

www.jungpage.org

www.psychoanalysis.org.uk/our-authors-and-theorists/donald-woods-winnicott

www.squiggle-foundation.org/winnicott/theories

www.thebowlbycentre.org.uk

www.simplypsychology.org/bowlby.html

www.simplypsychology.org/mary-ainsworth.html

www.schematherapysociety.org/Schema-Therapy

www.schemainstitute.co.uk/understanding-schema-therapy

DBS Update Service

www.gov.uk/dbs-update-service

Safeguarding Resources

www.samaritans.org/how-we-can-help/if-youre-worried-about-someone-else/supporting-someone-suicidal-thoughts/creating-safety-plan

www.papyrus-uk.org

Printed in Great Britain
by Amazon